Cambridge Elements ≡

Elements in Quantitative and Computational Methods
for the Social Sciences
edited by
R. Michael Alvarez
California Institute of Technology
Nathaniel Beck
New York University

AGENT-BASED MODELS
OF SOCIAL LIFE

Fundamentals

Michael Laver

New York University

CAMBRIDGE
UNIVERSITY PRESS

University Printing House, Cambridge CB2 8BS, United Kingdom

One Liberty Plaza, 20th Floor, New York, NY 10006, USA

477 Williamstown Road, Port Melbourne, VIC 3207, Australia

314–321, 3rd Floor, Plot 3, Splendor Forum, Jasola District Centre,
New Delhi – 110025, India

79 Anson Road, #06–04/06, Singapore 079906

Cambridge University Press is part of the University of Cambridge.

It furthers the University's mission by disseminating knowledge in the pursuit of
education, learning, and research at the highest international levels of excellence.

www.cambridge.org
Information on this title: www.cambridge.org/9781108796200
DOI: 10.1017/9781108854665

First published 2020

A catalogue record for this publication is available from the British Library.

ISBN 978-1-108-79620-0 Paperback
ISSN 2398-4023 (online)
ISSN 2514-3794 (print)

Additional resources for this publication at www.cambridge.org/laver1.

Agent-Based Models of Social Life

Fundamentals

Elements in Quantitative and Computational Methods
for the Social Sciences

DOI: 10.1017/9781108854665
First published online: March 2020

Michael Laver
New York University
Author for correspondence: ml127@nyu.edu

Abstract: Social interactions are rich, complex, and dynamic. One way to understand these is to model interactions that fascinate us. Some of the more realistic and powerful models are computer simulations. Simple, elegant, and powerful tools are available in user-friendly free software to help you design, build, and run your own models of social interactions that intrigue you, and do this on the most basic laptop computer. Focusing on a well-known model of housing segregation, this Element is about how to unleash that power, setting out the fundamentals of what is now known as agent-based modeling.

Keywords: agent-based models, social interaction, segregation, simulation

ISBNs: 9781108796200 (PB), 9781108854665(OC)
ISSNs: 2398-4023 (online), 2514-3794 (print)

Contents

Code files for all named NetLogo models (set in bold text) referred to in this Element are available at
www.cambridge.org/laver1.

1 Introduction

Social interactions are rich, complex, dynamic – and endlessly fascinating. One way to understand them is to design and build theoretical models of interactions that fascinate us. Some of the more realistic and powerful models are computer simulations. The good news is that simple, elegant, and powerful tools are available right now to help you design and build your own simulations of the social world. Even better news is that these tools are easily available in user-friendly free software. This software allows you design, build and run your own theoretical model of any social interaction that intrigues you. And you can do all this on the most basic laptop computer. The ability to build powerful computer models of social interaction, once the preserve of a privileged few, has moved down to street level. This Element is about how to unleash that power to develop and explore your own theoretical ideas about how the world works.

Computer models of social interaction typically analyze the behavior of autonomous artificial agents. Each agent is a simulated human decision maker with actions determined by computer code written by the model builder – by you. Each agent has its own brain (referring to agents using the gender-blind "it") and *each agent's brain is designed by you*! In simple models, you might program all your agents' brains to have exactly the same response in the same situation, as if the real humans you model were all clones of each other. Since real humans are not all clones of each other, however, you can easily program different types of agent to respond to the same situation in different ways. Such diversity is at the heart of human interaction. You will already be well aware that real-world social interactions typically evolve into settings where very different types of people coexist side by side.

After you have programmed your agents' brains, specifying their responses to changes in their environment and encounters with other agents, you hit the "go" button and set your model running. You can then sit back and observe, record, and analyze the resulting social dynamics. Computers never get tired, so you can go to bed and run the model overnight if you want to see how things evolve over the very long run. You can run your model for weeks until your laptop smokes and glue runs out of its seams.

The beauty of all of this is that you, the model's author, have great freedom to develop and explore your own theories of social interaction, programming your agents to behave in ways you think are interesting and instructive. You can also take anyone else's theoretical model and adapt it to take account of your own ideas. This is why what is now known as agent-based modeling is so downright addictive – pure fun that at the same time allows you to investigate theoretical ideas about social interaction in a way that goes far beyond the capabilities of most alternative approaches.

My aim in what follows is to seduce you into designing and programming your own agent-based models (ABMs) of social interactions that fascinate you. We'll get your models up and running, then see how to exercise them in a careful way that lets you draw confident conclusions about social interaction. Everyone is a theorist in their own head, but the gold standard is to develop theoretical models that are widely accessible to others yet rigorous in the sense that different people, using the same model in the same way, see the same results.

My approach in this Element is hands-on. You'll be encouraged from the very start to design, program, and run theoretical models that address social interactions you care about. The modeling platform we use to do this is NetLogo, a stable and intuitive programming environment, available as a free download at http://ccl.northwestern.edu/netlogo. It's also important that NetLogo is public domain, open source software (https://github.com/NetLogo/NetLogo). Code files for all named NetLogo models (set in bold text) referred to in this Element are available at www.cambridge.org/laver1. NetLogo's greatest virtue is that it is both simple and powerful. Some who work with ABMs are coding ninjas who like work as close as possible to the bare metal of the machine, valuing raw speed above all else. But a core value of this Element and of NetLogo is that ABMs are for everyone and should be as transparent and accessible as possible. The computer code powering them must be legible to anyone with just a modicum of effort. Having built a shiny new model of some important social interaction, what you want above all else is for as many people as possible not only to admire it, *but to use and understand it*. You want others to modify, improve, extend, and, yes, criticize it. Your ideal is that your theoretical model provokes vigorous and wide-ranging discussion. Agent-based modeling is transformative precisely because it puts a powerful modeling technology into the hands of so many people – democratizing social theory in the process. It should be inclusive, not exclusive, and the way to achieve this is to make tools that are as accessible as possible. NetLogo does this.

Depending on your interests and expertise, you may eventually run up against the limits of NetLogo and feel the need for fancier software. If you like to code in Python, for example, you'll find a Python ABM framework at https://pypi.org/project/Mesa/. I'm a simple person, holding the view that if it's too complicated for NetLogo, it's too complicated. For many reasons we'll discover later, fancier models are often worse models. I wrote a book-length treatment of party competition as an evolving, complex system using nothing but NetLogo. NetLogo will get you a very long way, and in my view its very simplicity encourages you to specify simpler and better models. Furthermore, if you ever feel you've reached the end of the road with NetLogo, you'll be well able to make your own software choices, and I will wish you all the best.

Plan of Campaign

This Element is the first of a two-part introduction to agent-based modeling. This part will hopefully take you from zero to ninety in agent-based modeling in as fast and friendly a way as possible. It assumes nothing about your prior experience with either modeling social interactions or writing computer code. Old hands at doing these things might be tempted to skim early sections. My humble suggestion is to read them anyway because agent-based modeling is different from other approaches to modeling social interaction, and writing code for agent-based models is different from other types of computer coding.

My aim is to have everyone writing NetLogo code for agent-based models as fluently as if they were writing in their own native tongue. I want you to be thinking about the theoretical *model* and the *problems* it addresses, not the *code*. This involves lots of hands-on work. We'll get our hands dirty right away by analyzing, torturing, and extending an early and influential model of social segregation designed by Thomas Schelling.[1] The core intuition from this model is that, if we have only a very mild preference for having people "like us" as neighbors but move house when we're unhappy with our neighborhood, then the resulting social interactions lead to the evolution of startlingly high levels of social segregation. We find ourselves living in *much more segregated neighborhoods than we want*. The Schelling model is simple and powerful – the best type of model – and you'll find a faithful rendition of it in the NetLogo models library.

Given its simplicity, accessibility, and power, I use the Schelling segregation model throughout the next five sections as a vehicle for learning about many aspects of designing and programming ABMs. In the next section we look at how the model was coded in NetLogo and play with it a little to get some basic intuitions. This is as far as many people get with agent-based models, treating them essentially as discovery toys. That's not a bad thing, but we'll be going a *great* deal further. In Section 3 we move beyond casual play to deploy the segregation model as a serious research tool. We do this by specifying a suite of computer simulations designed to exercise and investigate the model, analyzing and presenting the results of these simulations, and drawing well-founded conclusions you would be happy to publish to the whole world.

---

[1] Schelling, T. 1971. "Dynamic models of segregation." *Journal of Mathematical Sociology* 1: 143–86.

After we have gotten serious with the baseline segregation model in Section 3, Section 4 moves on to consider how we might improve and extend it. The baseline model everyone has been talking about for years has only two social groups, treats all agents as clones of each other, and considers only hyperlocal social neighborhoods. What if there are more groups? Or if different agents have different preferences? Or if social neighborhoods are more extensive? Would these improvements change longstanding core intuitions from the Schelling model? The great beauty of ABM is that it's a simple matter to modify and reinterrogate this famous model in search of systematic answers. When you've read previous theoretical accounts of social interaction you may well have thought, "What about this, or that?" Now, using ABM, you can derive your own rigorous answers to such questions.

Indeed, this is why agent-based modeling is such a potent tool for anyone interested in theorizing about social interactions. It's one thing to develop a nice, simple, and plausible theory about some social interaction and then speculate about ways this might be extended. But the *great* advantage of computationally powered theory is that you must be *very* precise about theoretical extensions before you can turn these into computer code. And you will often find that the theoretical extension you were thinking about is rather woolly and vague, looking quite different when you make it precise enough to code. The need to program your agents' brains in a very precise way is a great source of discipline when you theorize about social interactions.

We will quickly find, as we extend it, that the baseline Schelling model is very path-dependent. In particular, as soon as all agents are happy with their locations, no agent ever moves again and model output reaches a stationary state. Each time agents stop moving because they're all happy, however, the configuration of their locations, the stationary state, is somewhat different. The real social world is a much more uncertain place, in which no stationary state persists forever. We take account of this in Section 5 by adding a random, or stochastic, component to the segregation model. This models the plain fact that at least *some* people move house for random reasons that have nothing at all to do with being unhappy with their local neighborhood. For example, they may get a new job in another city, cross the country to care for a sick relative, or move for many other reasons. We model this randomness by giving agents some small probability of looking for a new location, even when they're happy with their local neighborhood. Adding this stochastic component changes the model in fundamental and desirable ways. Not only does it make the model more realistic but, since some agents are always moving, the model never stops in an arbitrary location. Since each agent now has some small probability of moving to any location in the NetLogo world, the model becomes much less path-dependent. Left running for a *very* long time, all run repetitions tend to converge on the same general outcome, no matter what the starting configuration of agent locations. It may seem counterintuitive when you first think about this, but adding some randomness to your model in this way is a good thing, because it can increase the tendency of outputs from different model run-repetitions to converge on each other. And this allows you to be more confident about the insights you derive from the model.

Up to this point, we extended the Schelling segregation model by adding new features in a well-disciplined way, one at a time. Each time we specified a new feature, we added this to the baseline model on its own so that we could carefully assess the effects of doing this. If what we want is the most realistic model we can achieve, however, we might well want to add many new features at the same time. We conclude this introduction to agent-based modeling, in Section 6, by combining several innovations we discussed into a single, more realistic model of social segregation. We quickly see that, while first instincts might favor deploying the most realistic model we can specify, more realistic models typically have more moving parts. Models with more moving parts, especially when these interact with each other, are typically much harder to understand. They may therefore be less fertile sources of intuition. If, however, we want our model to help us estimate something important about a particular real-world setting, such as where a particular hurricane is most likely to make landfall, we above all want our model to be as realistic as possible. We may then well be prepared to pay a price for this in lost intuitions about the interactions we are modeling. We conclude this Element, therefore, by thinking about a trade-off between realism and intuition, which lies at the very heart of the modeling enterprise.

I finish this section with an observation that may seem geeky, but which informs these Elements and may interest those concerned with the distinction between computational theories of social life, like the ones we explore later, and the formal or logical theories more often found in economics or political science. There is a longstanding argument linking computer science and logic, known as the Curry-Howard isomorphism. Simply put, this says that a computer program is essentially a logical proof, and a logical proof is essentially a program for deriving a result. Both are sets of logical statements that imply a particular outcome or outcomes. Google this topic and read up on it if this argument interests you, but the overall point is not to obsess about this distinction. Contrary to what some who don't know much about ABMs may think, an ABM is an analytical model of the world, logically resolved by the computer code and research design that express it. If you take ABM seriously, you will generate results every bit as true as propositions derived mathematically from formal models. These Elements are about helping you do that.

2 Social Segregation: Basics

The Core Intuition

When people belong to social groups that are important to them for some reason or another, we often see the evolution of local neighborhoods where most people live surrounded by others of the same group. The tendency to associate with similar others, called homophily, can generate a pervasive pattern of geographic social segregation. The surprising and disturbing thing about how this segregation evolves is that, even when people have only a mild preference for living close to others like themselves but move to another location if this mild preference is not satisfied, they often find themselves living in *much* more segregated neighborhoods than they really want.

Nobel Prize winner Thomas Schelling developed one of the first agent-based models of this important social phenomenon. He did this before the era of personal computers, "running" his model by moving pieces by hand around a large checkerboard that functioned, just like an abacus, as a physical computer. His model adapts very well to modern electronic computers, and there is a faithful implementation (called Segregation) in the NetLogo models library.[2] Look for the models library in the NetLogo "file" menu and find the Segregation model, along with many other nice models, in the library's "Social Science" folder. This model is beautiful, being both very simple and very powerful, and will therefore be a real pleasure for us to use as a vehicle for learning about ABM.

We're going to learn by doing, so let's find out about the Schelling segregation model by jumping right in and running it. Download the model from the NetLogo models library. Open it. Hit the "setup" button. The top panel of Figure 2.1 shows what you see. The big multicolored square to the right of the screen is the NetLogo world. In this model, the world represents a geographic area, say all or part of a city. The little squares inside it represent places, called patches in NetLogo, where people might live. Black patches are unoccupied. Agents belonging to one of two social groups, red and green, live on colored patches. There are approximately equal numbers of red and green agents, and when you hit the "setup" button you scatter these randomly around the patches in the NetLogo world. Keep hitting "setup" and you see a different random scattering of red and green agents, but always about the same number of each.

Now hit the "go" button and set the model in motion. Watch agents move as they sort themselves into more or less segregated neighborhoods – much more

---

[2] Wilensky, U. 1997. NetLogo Segregation model. http://ccl.northwestern.edu/netlogo/models/ Segregation. Center for Connected Learning and Computer-Based Modeling, Northwestern University, Evanston, IL.

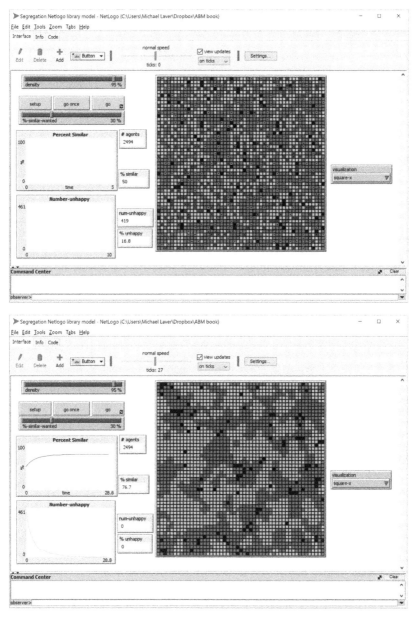

Figure 2.1 Screen shots from the default NetLogo implementation of the Schelling segregation model, before (top panel) and after (bottom panel) a model run

segregated than their random start. The bottom panel of Figure 2.1 shows an example of what might happen. (It may happen quite fast on your computer. To see it in slow motion, go to the "normal speed" slider above the NetLogo world and drag it toward the left.) The greenish-blue slider called `%-similar-wanted` shows that agents in this model want 30 percent of their neighbors to belong to the same social group as themselves. (I distinguish NetLogo code and variables from other text by `printing them in a font like this`.) The beige `% similar` monitor and `Percent Similar` plot show what happens when agents move house whenever fewer than 30 percent of their neighbors belong to the same social group and keep moving until this preference is satisfied. This is the simple but powerful logical engine of the Schelling segregation model. For the example in the bottom panel of Figure 2.1, people who want just 30 percent of their neighbors to come from the same group as themselves, and move whenever they don't find this, end up living in much more segregated neighborhoods where about 76 percent of their neighbors belong to the same group. This is Schelling's core theoretical intuition, one that has been extremely influential in many different settings since it was first published.

Hit the "setup" and "go" buttons until you're exhausted and you always see something a bit different but nonetheless quite similar, *always* involving the evolution of segregated neighborhoods. The more times you do this, the more confident you are about the core intuition: people who behave as Schelling assumes sort themselves into much more segregated neighborhoods than they want. This, albeit in a very simple form, is *exactly* how you derive reliable theoretical conclusions from an ABM. Random things happen. So, outcomes of different model run repetitions, like outcomes in the real world, are never precisely the same. Here, this happens because there are random (stochastic) elements in the model, which we'll shortly consider. Nonetheless, randomness in both the model and the real world does not prevent us from drawing reliable conclusions about important patterns in social behavior.

We just saw that the NetLogo implementation delivers the core intuition of the Schelling ABM of social segregation. What you really want to do is modify this model to test your own ideas about the evolution of social segregation. First, however, we must find our way around NetLogo. Go back to the NetLogo screens in Figure 2.1. Near the top of each you'll see three tabs: "Interface," "Info," and "Code." The "Interface" tab is selected, and you've already been working with the interface when you hit "setup" and "go." We'll be returning in more detail to this. The "Info" tab shows lots of information about the computer model, supplied by the model's author. Read this to find out what is going on and see suggestions of things you might do with the model. The "Code" tab contains the NetLogo code that runs the model. You can see at once that the language of this code is close to English. Once you get used to it, you'll read NetLogo code almost as easily as you're reading this sentence. Think of NetLogo as a power tool. The interface is what you see and use on a daily basis, the code is the internal (logical) engine, and the "getting started" manual is in the info tab.

We're now going to break all the rules and tinker with the engine before we even read the manual, just to see how easy it is to code in NetLogo. Look at the NetLogo world on the interface and you will see, immediately *after* you hit setup and *before* you hit go, that some little squares have an "x" in them and some do not. The squares with an "x" show unhappy agents who plan to move. The squares with no "x" show happy agents who plan to stay right where they are. This is rather boring, so let's give happy agents a smiley face and unhappy agents a sad face. This is easy, if rather silly. Click the "Code" tab and peer at the logical engine. Find the procedure called to update-turtles. It's in some lines of code near the bottom, of which the first is to update-turtles and the last is end. (We'll soon discuss procedures, which always begin with to and end with end.) Shortly before end you'll see the following line of code:

```
ifelse happy? [set shape "square"] [set shape "square-x"]
```

The ifelse instruction is a logical fork in the road and is very useful in both NetLogo and other coding environments. It tells the machine, "If the following condition is satisfied, carry out the first instruction that follows; else, carry out the second instruction." The condition here is happy? and the code tells NetLogo, "If the agent is happy, show it as a square; else show it as a square with an 'x' in it." Replace square with face happy and replace square-x with face sad. That gives you:

```
ifelse happy? [set shape "face happy"] [set shape "face sad"]
```

Click the green "Check" button at the top of the code to make sure you haven't made a mistake. This catches most typos. Go back to the interface tab and hit "setup." Instead of squares you see happy and sad faces. Hit "go" and see the agents move around until they all have happy faces. You're now successfully coding in NetLogo! Fresh from this minor triumph, let's get more familiar with the NetLogo modeling environment. Before doing anything else, however, save your modified model under a new name, such as **Segregation 1.01 faces.**

VERSION CONTROL ALERT!

If you want to save your smiley face model before moving on, use "save as" in the file menu and *give it a new name*, such as "Segregation model with faces."

Never, ever, ever, **overwrite your original model with code changes!**
You *always* want to be able to go back to the original when something goes wrong, and, sooner or later, something *will* go wrong.

Now, go back to the baseline model you downloaded from the NetLogo models library and make a copy called "Segregation 1.0." Every time you change this model, save it as "Segregation 1.1," "Segregation 1.2," and so on. When you make a really big change that generates a different version of the model, you can proudly celebrate this by saving it as "Segregation 2.0," "Segregation 2.1," and so on.

This practice may seem overcautious but, trust me, a time will come when you will be *really* glad you did this. It will save you untold hours of exasperation and misery.

The NetLogo World

We have already seen the NetLogo world in the Segregation model, the big square to the right of the interface tab. This is a rectangular grid of patches, small squares that combine to make up the world inhabited by NetLogo's artificial agents. You can give these patches all sorts of properties that define the environment in which your agents live. Different patches may supply different amounts of energy, for example, or different levels of danger or difficulty. We'll come back to all that later. Depending on what you want to model, this world may be a physical space, as in the segregation model. ABMs often do have a physical geography, distinguishing them from other models of social interaction, which often have no geography. In the Schelling segregation model, agents have physical neighbors – people who live close by – and they are more likely to interact with neighbors than with those who live farther away.

The NetLogo model world can also be a conceptual space. For example, in some of the sections in the second of the two Elements, we'll think of horizontal and vertical dimensions not as east-west and north-south, but as "left- versus right-wing" preferences on economic issues, or "liberal versus conservative" preferences on social issues. And you don't need to give your model any geography at all, whether physical or conceptual. Because geography does structure many social interactions in the real world, however, it's nice that you can easily take this into account in NetLogo. Click the "settings" button over the NetLogo world. Figure 2.2 shows what you see.

We're mostly interested in the top half of this panel. First, you see that the world is 51 patches wide and 51 patches high, 2601 patches in all. This value is an odd number because positions in the NetLego world in this particular example are

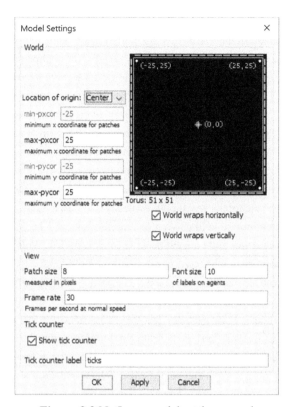

Figure 2.2 NetLogo model settings panel

described by a coordinate system that has (0, 0) as its origin and ranges from –25 to +25 both horizontally and vertically – just like latitude and longitude in our physical world. This coordinate system is completely under your control. You can shrink or expand the world horizontally or vertically by changing max-pxcor and max-pycor. These are two NetLogo variables that set the maximum size of the world. Try that now. You can fix things so that the origin is not at the center, if that's what you want. You do this using the "location of origin" chooser. You will now be able to change the NetLogo variables min-pxcor and min-pycor. Try that too.

The default NetLogo world is 33 by 33 patches, which I find a little lacking in detail. The NetLogo world for the Segregation model is 51 by 51 patches, which I find to be a good sweet spot, since it allows quite a bit of detail while also letting the model run fast on most machines. If you desperately feel your model needs more patches (although you'll rarely really need a higher level of detail), you can get these at the stroke of a key by increasing max-pxcor and max-pycor. Your more detailed model will run slower, however, so you'll be less able to explore it – a classic trade-off in all computational work.

Next, and crucially, see the green border around the world. Below the world are two checked boxes saying "World wraps horizontally" and "World wraps vertically." This is a model artifact – something we wish didn't happen but is unavoidable when we squash the near-infinite world in which we live into the finite world of a computer. The key question concerns what happens when you get to the edge of the world? Do you fall off, do you bounce back, or do you keep on going as if the world had no edge? We humans don't have to worry about this because we've yet to find the edge of our world and have no idea what happens when we get there. But the computer's memory, and therefore any world simulated in a computer, is finite, even if you have a monster computer with an enormous memory. Modelers usually choose to "wrap" the model world both vertically and horizontally, as in this case. This is almost, but not quite like living on a perfect sphere – keep walking in the same direction, and you find yourself back where you started. Wrapping the world horizontally means that, when agents march off the right-hand edge of the screen, they appear on the left-hand edge at precisely the same vertical position. When they march off the top, they appear at the bottom at precisely the same horizontal position. The model world actually has the shape of a ring donut, technically a torus, which is the word you see beneath the world in Figure 2.2.

If you uncheck the "world wrap" boxes, you see a red line round your world, boxing your agents in. When they hit the edge of the world, they won't fall off and die; they'll bounce back in just as if they were balls hitting the edge of a pool table. Most modelers agree that having agents bounce off the world's edge like balls on a pool table is a very unrealistic model artifact, known as an edge effect. Another edge effect of boxing agents in the segregation model is that not all of them have the same number of adjacent patches. Most can have up to eight neighbors, but agents in the corners can have only three, and agents at edges, but not corners, only five. This model artifact has a significant impact on how the model runs and is something we really want to avoid. To avoid undesirable edge effects, therefore, most models wrap their world like a torus. If you don't want your agents eventually reappearing back where they started when they keep walking in a horizontal or vertical line, then you can make your model world big enough, or program your agents so that this doesn't happen. But wrapping your world into a torus usually works pretty well, however odd this might seem at first sight.

The Model Interface

Click the "Interface" tab to access the model's interface, shown in Figure 2.1 for the Segregation model fresh out of the box. The interface does many useful things. First, it shows you what the model is doing as it runs. We have already seen how agents move around as the model runs and the model world evolves. The blue-gray buttons marked "setup," "go once," and "go" set the model in motion. Hitting one of these buttons runs part of the model's code, and you can put any button you like on the interface to run any code you want. Right-click on the "setup" button and choose "edit." You'll see that the button runs the procedure `setup` in the model's code, and it displays the name "setup." The procedure `setup` does everything in the `to setup` procedure in the model's code. We'll come to that soon. If you want to call the button something more exciting than "setup," replace the display name "setup" with "hi there, let's get started!" That works, though you'll find that the button grows way too large to hold all that text and that you'll irritate other users. Most modelers choose "setup" as a name for this type of procedure, and your code will be more legible to others if you do the same. Resize or move the setup button by right-clicking and selecting it. You can now resize and drag the button around the interface.

The "go" button is slightly different, but in a very important way. It's got two little arrows on it, which make it a "forever" button. When you click a forever button, the button goes black and the relevant model code runs not just once but over and over again *forever* until you click the button again. Actually, the `go` procedure in the Segregation model cleverly stops itself when all agents are happy, so it doesn't run forever. But we can knock that out and see what happens. Click the code tab and look at the code for `to go`. It's just under the setup code. You'll see the instruction `if all? turtles [happy?] [stop]`. Stripping out the odd-looking punctuation and noting that NetLogo's generic agents are (unfortunately) called "turtles," it's obvious what that means: stop if all agents are happy. You can snip that line out of the code by doing one of two things: (1) You can simply delete it. This is *very* bad coding practice when you're developing a model, though it would be fine for a lean and mean final version of the code. So don't do that. *Much* better is (2) to turn this line of code into a comment. You'll see in the code that some lines start with a semicolon, ";" and appear in gray. These lines are comments. They're not part of the model's code but comments from the code's author telling readers what the code is doing. We'll spend more time on comments later, but for now we present the following coding tip.

Coding Tip! Commenting Out

When experimenting with a new model or trying to diagnose some problem with the code, a useful trick is to "comment out" lines of code rather than deleting them.

Do this in NetLogo by putting a semicolon at the beginning of lines of code you want to comment out.

This has exactly the same effect as deleting the code, but it's much clearer what you've done if things go wrong – as they will – and the old code is still there if you want to restore it.

Be very careful that the line(s) of code you comment out have a stand-alone effect on the model. If they have an impact on other parts of the code (for example, changing a variable), then your code may crash or, worse, not crash but generate misleading results.

So type ";" in front of `if all? turtles [happy?] [stop]` and watch the line of code go gray. You've commented this line out. Hit the green "check" button to see that you've done nothing mad, bad, or dangerous. Now return to the interface and hit `setup` and `go`. The interface looks just the same as before, except that now the model never stops running. The `go` button stays black, and the tick counter above the world at the top left, which counts the number of times you've cycled through the model, just keeps on going. All agents are happy, but the model keeps asking them, "Are you unhappy? Would you like to move?" It will do this forever, no matter how many times all agents reply they are indeed happy, since you hit a forever button and never told the model to stop.

Normally you can get out of this pickle by just hitting the go button again to stop the go code in a perfectly orderly way. This works well in the present case, so go back to the code tab and "uncomment" the line that helpfully stops the model, doing this by deleting the ";" you just inserted. However, see the following tip.

CODING TIP! CRASH LANDINGS

Occasionally, when you're developing a new model, the code will start running but won't stop because of some diabolical coding error that sends it into an infinite loop (sooner or later you'll surely make one of these mistakes).

As a last resort you can force your model to crash land rather than running forever by going to the "tools" menu and choosing "halt." This, however, is a last resort. Always program your model to start and stop in an orderly way.

In addition to buttons the NetLogo model interface has greenish-blue sliders. The Segregation model's interface has two of these: `density` and `%-similar-wanted`. Sliders let you use the interface to change values of model parameters. These are variables that affect how the model runs. We'll look only at the `density` slider for now. Out of the box the model sets the model parameter `density` at 95 percent. This means that *on average* agents occupy 95 percent of the NetLogo world's patches, while 5 percent are

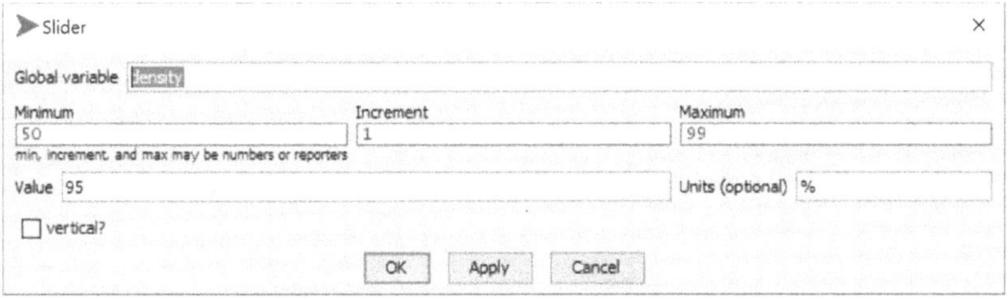

Figure 2.3 Segregation model default density slider

unoccupied. You can change that value by moving the slider. Left-click and slide it down to 75 percent. Now hit `setup`. You'll see many more unoccupied black patches. Maybe that makes a difference in how the model works – something we'll look at in the next section. Slide `density` down to 50 percent and you'll see many more empty patches. Whoever wrote the model didn't want you to go below 50 percent density, but we can fix that too.

To see how the `density` slider works and change it to do what you want, right-click it and hit "edit." Figure 2.3 shows what you see. The most important thing is that this slider sets the value of a global model variable called `density`. (A global variable, as we'll soon see, is a variable that can affect anything and everything in the model.) Below this, you see that the slider has a minimum value of 50 and a maximum of 99, the units being "%," and that the default value is 95 percent. You can change those limits to be anything you want, but as we'll see, some settings of `density` are so crazy they crash the model, some are crazy but don't crash the model (which is actually worse), and some are just plain uninteresting. The model's author picked an interesting range of `density` as the defaults. This is an important part of modeling called *calibration*, and we'll be giving a lot of thought to this down the line.

Meanwhile, to see exactly how the density slider works, we'll prize open the model and look at its code. Click the code tab and find the `setup` procedure. It's near the top of the code, but a quick way to find any procedure in NetLogo is to use the "procedures" chooser just above the code. This is great when there's a lot of code, so let's use that to find `setup`. This is what you see:

```
to setup
  clear-all
  ;; create turtles on random patches.
  ask patches [
    if random 100 < density [  ;; set the occupancy density
      sprout 1 [
        set color one-of [red green]
      ]
```

```
    ]
  ]
  update-turtles
  update-globals
  reset-ticks
end
```

Every procedure in NetLogo starts with to, followed by the procedure name, and finishes with end. Otherwise, it won't work. The green check tick will tell you this right away. Delete the end of the setup procedure and click check. You'll get a yellow error message: "END expected." NetLogo is not like a search engine, which does its best to insert end where it thinks you might want it. Where end goes makes a massive difference in how the code runs, and you, the model's author, must be the person who puts it there. So put end back where it belongs and hit the check button again to be sure you're back in business. In the code, clear-all and reset-ticks at the beginning and end of the procedure are bits of important boilerplate you'll find in any setup procedure. They simply clean up everything from the previous run and ready things for the next. We'll come back later to update-turtles and update-globals.

After clear-all we see the helpful comment ;;create turtles on random patches. (Remember, comments in NetLogo code are always preceded with a ";". NetLogo coders often use a double ";;" for extra legibility.) You're going to have to get used to the fact that NetLogo's default name for an artificial agent is turtle. The reasons for this go back into the mists of time, but you can console yourself by knowing you can rename your agents to whatever you want if calling them turtles gives you indigestion. We've been told in the comment that the code that follows is going to create agents on random patches, which is a vital part of our model. After the second comment is edited out, we have the following code that does this:

```
ask patches [
        if random 100 < density [
          sprout 1 [
            set color one-of [red green]
          ]
        ]
      ]
```

There's a lot to take on board here. First, note the varying indentation of the different lines of code. Putting code on different lines and indenting these is something coders do to increase legibility. It's a common style choice and considered good coding practice, but you don't need to do this to make the code run correctly. NetLogo would execute the following line of code in exactly the same way:

```
ask patches [if random 100 < density [sprout 1 [set color one-of [red green]]]]
```

It would just be harder for you, the reader, to figure out what was going on.

Note that, as far as NetLogo is concerned, *patches are agents too*! They can't move around like other agents, and as we have seen, they make up the environment of the NetLogo world. But you can ask them to do many things, like grow grass, supply votes, store mineral deposits, and much more besides. This gives you a lot of power over the NetLogo world. Here, we ask each patch to consider "sprouting" (creating) a new agent. The probability that any given patch sprouts a new agent is set by the `density` variable in the interface.

Having created new agents, we put each at random into one of two groups, red and green. The probabilistic creation of new agents, and their random assignment to groups, gives the model two random (stochastic) components before you even set it running. *On average*, 95 percent (more generally, "density" percent, whatever the value of `density` is) of patches will create a new agent, and *on average* red and green groups will be of equal size. But every time you hit the setup button, you'll create a slightly different number of agents, putting them in groups of slightly different sizes. This is just the same as what happens when you toss a coin. If you toss a coin ten times, then, on average, over many trials you'll get five heads and five tails. But this will surely not happen in every trial; there will be stochastic variation in the number of heads and tails from trial to trial. As we'll see down the line, random components such as these are absolutely crucial in allowing you to draw systematic conclusions from multiple runs of your model.

Going back to the code, this "asks" patches to do something. What it asks them is in the code between the matching square brackets starting with " [" and, crucially, finishing with "] ".

CODING TIP! ALWAYS MATCH BRACKETS

If you put " [" in NetLogo code, you're starting something that you MUST finish with "] ". The number of closing brackets "] " must always equal the number of opening brackets " [". It's easy to lose track of this, which is going to be one of your most common coding errors. Check this first if your code doesn't run.

The expression `random 100` picks a random *integer* between 0 and 99 (the largest integer *strictly less than* 100). The value of the `density` global is read from the interface and is 95 in the out-of-the-box implementation. The code `if random 100 < density` in this case compares a random integer between 0 and 99 with 95. If the integer is less than this value (which it usually will be), then the patch carries out the instruction(s) between the square brackets that follow. These are nested inside the first set of square brackets. The instruction tells the patch to `sprout 1`, that is, to create one new agent at its own location. You can create more than one agent on each patch by replacing "1" with the desired number of new agents. The new agent is now given instructions inside *yet another* set of square brackets, making three sets nested inside each other to keep track of. The instruction in this case is `set color one-of [red green]`. This is more or less self-explanatory, telling the agent to pick *at random* one of the colors in the list inside the (fourth set of) square brackets. We now carefully close all open (unmatched) square brackets, and we're done. (Keeping track of these brackets is a good reason to put them on different indented lines in the code.)

COMPUTERS AND RANDOM NUMBERS

Computer instructions, including some we just used, may refer to random numbers.

True random numbers are absolutely *unpredictable*; they appear in *sequences* that are absolutely unpredictable and *never repeat*. Computers can use true random numbers only if these come from an external *physical* source, such as atmospheric noise.

(If you really need true random numbers, a good supply is at www.random.org.)

When computers generate random numbers internally, as with NetLogo, they use an algorithm that outputs *pseudorandom* numbers. Modern pseudorandom number generators output numbers that are effectively indistinguishable from true random numbers. A sequence of pseudorandom numbers will repeat over the *extremely* long run, however, so is not truly random. But the period of this repetition is so long that it is of no practical concern.

Pseudorandom number generators start with a seed, such as a very high precision reading from the computer's system clock. Different seeds generate different sequences of pseudorandom numbers. *The same seed always generates the same sequence of numbers.*

This is actually a very valuable property for computer modeling, since a model with a stochastic component generates *exactly* the same output every time the same seed is used. If no seed is specified, the computer picks its own seed using the system clock; every run with a stochastic component then generates different output.

If you want to replicate a NetLogo model run *perfectly*, therefore, despite the fact it has a stochastic component, you can set the random seed yourself with the instruction random-seed abcdevwxyz, where abcdevwxyz is a number supplied by you. Every time you set the same seed for the same code, you get *exactly* the same output.

There are situations (e.g., if you want to replicate a particular model run perfectly) in which this feature of pseudorandom numbers is very useful.

Now we've seen what the density slider does, we see that you can easily give density crazy values that make no sense. Sometimes these will crash the code. Sometimes the code will just go ahead and do the crazy thing you asked, since the code always assumes you mean precisely what you say. An easy way to see this is to exploit another nice feature of the NetLogo interface, the command center at the bottom of the interface screen. You're the boss, the "observer" in NetLogo terms, and you can type and execute any valid NetLogo command on the command line labeled "observer>". Go to the command center and type set density 200 on the command line. This makes no sense; values of density must logically lie between 0 and 100 percent. Hit return and watch the density slider hop up to 200 percent. Hit setup and you won't get an error. This is because, when density = 200, NetLogo happily executes if random 100 < density. Obviously, the expression will always be true, and every single patch will generate a new agent, leaving no unoccupied patch. Now hit go. Nothing will happen, since there is no unoccupied patch for unhappy agents to move to, but the program will run forever. This is an unfortunate type of coding error because it doesn't alert you by crashing the code, which carries on happily as if nothing were wrong. You only see that bad things are happening by looking at the output and noticing that something is obviously wrong.

Contrast this with what happens if you type set density -200 into the command line. Hit return and nothing happens; the code has executed set density -200 despite the fact this is nonsensical. But now hit setup and see how the code crashes in flames, giving you a "division by zero" error message. This is because random 100 < density is impossible if density = -200. If you're a cautious coder, you can prevent this from happening by inserting error traps into the code – we'll come back to these later.

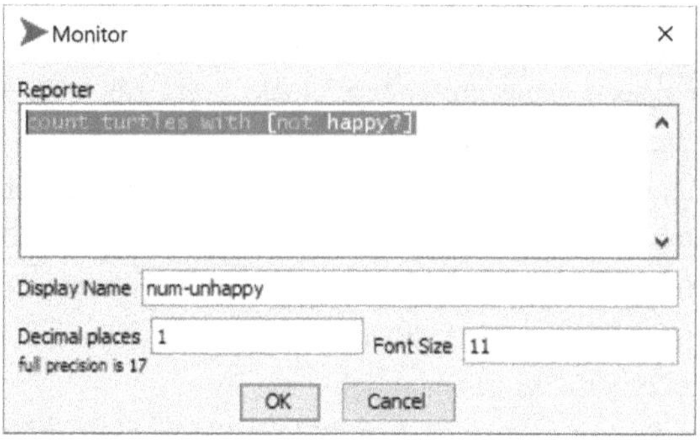

Figure 2.4 Segregation model "num-unhappy" monitor

The other things you'll find on this interface are blue-gray "choosers" and beige "monitors" and graphs. We'll come back to graphs later because they're a little tricky. Choosers are just like sliders, setting the values of global variables in the code. This time, however, the values are categories (colors, for example), not numbers. The chooser lets you pick a category. The monitors simply tell you the value of some quantity or variable in the code. The most complicated one here is "num-unhappy." Right-click this and pick "edit." Figure 2.4 shows what you see. The monitor called "num-unhappy" shows the number of unhappy turtles, by running the code `count turtles with [not happy?]` and reporting the result.

We learn something else new here. NetLogo has true/false variables (called Boolean variables), which are identified by having a "?" at the end of their name. As we will soon see, the variable `happy?` stores a property of individual agents and has the value "true" if the agent is happy, else "false." So `count turtles with [not happy?]` returns the number of unhappy agents – those for which the value of `happy?` is false.

Having found our way around the NetLogo interface and peeked at bits of the segregation model code, we can look at the Schelling segregation model in its full glory. As we do this, we'll also discover a lot about coding ABMs in NetLogo and, indeed, coding more generally. So click the "code" tab.

Variable Types

The first thing you *always* do when coding a new model is declare the variables you'll be using. These variables have different types when you're programming an ABM. Some apply to the whole world, some belong to particular agents. Keeping this straight is a *very* important part of programming an ABM.

One type of variable is a global. Global variables hold information about the NetLogo model world as a whole, and all agents know their values. Globals are "owned" by you, the coder (whom NetLogo calls the observer). They may be important inputs to, or outputs from, the model, and you can use them to direct the flow of the model and instruct agents. The observer can set the value of global variables directly but cannot ask an individual agent to do this. We'll soon see a global variable, percent-unhappy. This holds an important model output, summarizing information about all agents. It measures the percentage of unhappy agents, those for whom happy? is not true.

Another type of variable is agent-specific, which can have different values for each agent. Agents own their own data, stored in their agent variables. A good example we've already seen is the Boolean (true/false) agent-specific variable happy? This records the happiness of an individual agent, an agent-specific variable since, as we all know, happiness varies from person to person and is not a feature of the world as a whole.

Using the wrong type of variable in a particular context is a *very* common source of ABM coding errors. For example, make a mistake by inserting the following code at the end of the setup procedure:

```
if happy? [ask turtles [set color yellow]]
```

This superficially looks OK but is a fatal error because the agent-specific variable happy? is not a global and doesn't apply to *you*, the observer. NetLogo alerts you to this mistake with an error message: "You can't use HAPPY? in an observer context because HAPPY? is turtle-only." Perhaps you meant to ask *all happy agents to turn yellow*, in which case you should have said:

```
ask turtles [if happy? [set color yellow]]
```

This uses exactly the same words, but the different word order changes everything. Computers are relentless logic engines, and you resolve coding errors like this with careful, logical thought. I guarantee you will make coding errors like this. I have – many times. In compensation you will also find the distinction between global and agent-specific variables extraordinarily useful.

Declaring Global Variables

There are two ways to declare global variables in NetLogo. One is on the NetLogo interface, the other is in the code. The very top of the segregation code reads as follows:

```
globals [
    percent-similar ;; on the average, what percent of a turtle's neighbors
                    ;; are the same color as that turtle?
    percent-unhappy ;; what percent of the turtles are unhappy?
]
```

This says that you are declaring the two global variables named between the square brackets: percent-similar and percent-unhappy. The meaning of these variables has been helpfully explained by the coder in comments preceded by ";;".

Going back to the interface, we see that three more global variables are declared simply by being put on the interface. These are density, which we looked at, and %-similar-wanted, which measures the percentage of an agent's local neighbors who must be from the same social group if the agent is to be happy? and therefore stay put. We'll come to this shortly. There is also a very boring categorical variable, called visualization, declared by a chooser. This switches the look of the NetLogo world between what you now see on the interface and what you would have seen if you had run earlier versions of the model (which, of course, is of no conceivable interest to you whatsoever). So there are five global variables in all, two declared in the code and three on the interface. If you fail to declare a global variable in one of these two ways but nonetheless try to use it in your code, then the code will crash and tell you it has no idea what you're talking about. NetLogo is not a digital personal assistant powered by artificial intelligence that will try and guess what you want if you express yourself poorly. NetLogo is extremely, maddeningly literal.

Declaring Agent-Specific Variables

Immediately below the declaration of globals in the code, you'll see the expression turtles-own, which declares agent-specific variables, which, as we have seen, are owned by, and can vary between, individual agents.

```
turtles-own [
  happy?        ;; for each turtle, indicates whether at least %-similar-wanted
                ;; percent of
                ;; that turtle's neighbors are the same color as the turtle
  similar-nearby ;; how many neighboring patches have a turtle with my color?
  other-nearby   ;; how many have a turtle of another color?
  total-nearby   ;; sum of previous two variables
]
```

You can't declare these on the interface. Four agent-specific variables are declared, once more explained in helpful comments from the coder. These variables deal with whether or not the agent is happy?, which as we will see is affected by the types of agent living on neighboring patches – information kept in the other three agent-specific variables. Before going further, therefore, we need to know about NetLogo neighborhoods.

NetLogo Neighborhoods

We've seen that the NetLogo world is a checkerboard of patches displayed on the interface. Each patch has neighbors, patches located close by. NetLogo has two built-in types of neighborhood for each patch. The first includes each of the eight surrounding patches, including those touching the patch at its corners. This is the *Moore neighborhood*, named after Edward Moore, a famous pioneer of this type of work. For any given agent, the NetLogo function neighbors reports the identities of its eight surrounding patches. This is the type of neighborhood used in the Schelling segregation model.

Functions such as this are what makes NetLogo an ideal ABM programming environment. You could write some boilerplate code designed, for example, to list the patches bordering any specified agent, but this would be tiresome and unfulfilling. NetLogo has done a lot of this boilerplate work for you, providing packages of code that do many useful things – some of these really quite complicated. You call these code packages using NetLogo functions. One of these functions is neighbors. If you want an agent to count the number of its neighboring agents, all you have to ask is: count turtles-on neighbors. You'll find, and very gratefully rely on, NetLogo functions for many of the things you'll want to do. You can get an excellent sense of the full range of NetLogo functions by opening any NetLogo model, going to the Help menu, and opening the NetLogo Dictionary. This explains hundreds of NetLogo functions and will be your main source of reference when coding in NetLogo, no matter how proficient you become. Take a peek at it now, though you shouldn't be downcast if it seems overwhelming. Be excited at the huge range of possibilities that open up for you as you steadily master NetLogo.

An alternative type of neighborhood comprises only the four patches that share a line boundary with the reference patch: those to the direct north, south, east, and west of it. This is the von Neumann neighborhood, named after John von Neumann, another pioneer of this type of modeling. The NetLogo function neighbors4 returns the identities of patches in the von Neumann neighborhood. It is easy to think of other types of neighborhood, code these in NetLogo, and use them in your models. When we dig deeper into this, we'll find that the type of neighborhood you specify makes a *big* difference to your results. We dramatically change output from the Schelling segregation model, for example, by changing the type of neighborhood we specify. So this is a very important modeling choice.

Central Control: The go Procedure

The go procedure in NetLogo, activated by the "go" button on the interface, is the control center of any ABM, containing the code that controls how the model runs. You might think this means the go procedure will be huge, but ideally it should be quite the opposite, containing just a few instructions that call key model procedures found elsewhere in the code. In theory you could load the entire model code into the go procedure, but in practice this would be a terrible idea. Your code will be much easier to understand, fix, and develop if it is broken down into self-contained modules, each contained in a well-specified procedure. What the go procedure then does is simply call the right procedures in the right order to make the model do what you want it to do.

The entire go procedure for the baseline Schelling segregation model is very simple:

```
to go
  if all? turtles [happy?] [stop]
  move-unhappy-turtles
  update-turtles
  update-globals
  tick
end
```

We already saw that the first line of code simply stops the model run rather than letting it run forever after all agents are happy? so that none will ever move again and nothing more can possibly happen. The tick immediately before end simply advances the model's tick counter, which records how many model cycles have happened since the counter was reset in the setup procedure. This is often important information. The model's remaining three lines of code simply call three model procedures: move-unhappy-turtles, update-turtles, and update-globals. Each cycle of the model implements each of these procedures in the order specified. *This order is utterly crucial.* You may sometimes find your model is either crashing or giving you crazy results because you got the order of procedures wrong. You need to think very carefully and logically about this order. Running the model means repeatedly running three procedures in sequence. So what do these procedures do?

GOOD CODING PRACTICE: MODULARIZE!

Write your code as if you're making Lego blocks, and then assemble these into the final model.

Whenever you want to do something that can be a self-contained module, like `move-unhappy-turtles`, write a separate procedure for this.

There may in turn be procedures inside procedures, like `find-new-spot`. If in doubt, put the code in a separate procedure.

This has many advantages over stuffing all your code into a single giant procedure.

First, the code will be much more structured and legible to others coming to this for the first time. It will also be more legible to your future self who, months or years from now, may well have forgotten the nitty-gritty of what you were trying to do way back when, but now needs to fix or extend something.

Second, and even more importantly, your model will be much easier to improve and extend if the model code is very modular. Most extensions and improvements relate to some particular module. The last thing you want to do is to tinker with the whole program, which may end badly. Rather, you want to make a particular change to a particular module, keeping everything else exactly the same, to see what systematic difference this makes to the model's output.

Core Model Procedures

The `move-unhappy-turtles` procedure is the logical engine of the segregation model. Good models typically have a clearly visible logical engine.

```
to move-unhappy-turtles
  ask turtles with [not happy?]
    [find-new-spot]
end
```

This asks unhappy agents to find a new place to call home. Recall that `happy?` is a Boolean agent variable that is "true" if the agent is happy and "false" otherwise; we'll come to what makes agents `happy?` in a moment. The instruction `ask turtles with [not happy?]` asks all agents for which the statement in square brackets is true to do something. If the agent is unhappy, then [not happy?] is true. What these unhappy agents are asked to do is contained in the next set of square brackets. In this case it is find-new-spot, a behavior specified in the following procedure:

```
to find-new-spot
    rt random-float 360
    fd random-float 10
    if any? other turtles-here [find-new-spot]
                            ;; keep going until we find an unoccupied patch
      move-to patch-here    ;; move to center of patch
end
```

Essentially, this code tells an unhappy agent to keep making random moves until it finds an empty spot. The instruction rt random-float 360 tells the agent to spin on the spot to face a new random heading; rt is short for right and asks the agent to turn to the right by random-float 360 degrees. The expression random-float 360 returns a random number with many decimal points that is zero or higher but strictly less than 360. (The computer is a finite machine and cannot store infinitely large numbers or numbers of infinitely high precision. It uses floating point, not real numbers, hence random-float.) Having spun on the spot, the agent is then told fd random-float 10. The instruction fd is short for forward, and random-float 10 picks a random distance that is zero or higher but strictly less than 10. The net result of these two instructions is that the unhappy agent picks a new spot at random from within a circle centered on its current location, with a radius of 10. Note that these are local random moves within a neighborhood, but one much bigger than the Moore neighborhood surrounding the agent, which is the source of its unhappiness. Using this type of neighborhood for the random moves is a substantive modeling choice that may or may not be realistic and may or may not make a difference to model output. Though this choice is not explicitly justified, there is an implicit theoretical assumption that, if possible, unhappy agents in the real world do not want to move too far from their current location. We could easily change this for much more elegant code that simply asks agents to go to a random empty patch anywhere in the world.

```
to find-new-spot
    move-to one-of patches with [not any? turtles-here]
end
```

The code move-to one-of patches asks the agent to move to a random patch; the qualifier one-of picks a random patch. The condition [not any? turtles-here] restricts this choice to empty patches. Now that we've reduced the procedure find-new-spot to a single line of code, we don't really need it to be a separate procedure. Simpler code is typically better, and we could simplify the code by deleting the procedure find-new-spot and modifying move-unhappy-turtles to give:

```
to move-unhappy-turtles
    ask turtles with [not happy?]
        [move-to one-of patches with [not any? turtles-here]]
end
```

The requirement that at most one agent can live on any patch, with no multiple occupancy of patches, is another theoretical modeling choice that is *substantively very important but buried in the code*, implemented by if any? other turtles-here [find-new-spot]. This is a complex (recursive) instruction in the find-new-spot procedure that tells the procedure to call itself again if the agent's random move lands on a patch already occupied by another agent. Having procedures call themselves is in my view bad practice and something you should only do with extreme care, if you want avoid sending the code into an infinite loop. Here, however, the original model coders got away with it.

The restriction preventing more than one agent from inhabiting any patch creates a situation in which housing density is uniform across the NetLogo world. There is no multiple occupancy; there are no high-density neighborhoods. If you think this is a bad description of modern cities, then *you can modify this with a single keystroke*. You do this by commenting out the instruction if any? other turtles-here [find-new-spot] by typing a ";" in front of the if. Now your model allows multiple occupancy and still runs perfectly! As we will see in Section 4, this leads to *completely* different levels of social segregation from those evolving under the baseline model, so this is a crucial modeling assumption.

If you want a lean, mean model with multiple occupancy and no restrictions on the movement of unhappy agents, then you can delete the find-new-spot procedure and replace the move-unhappy-turtles procedure with the simple and intuitive:

```
to move-unhappy-turtles
    ask turtles with [not happy?] [move-to one-of patches]
end
```

As a general rule, your model should be as simple and transparent as possible, introducing complications only if you have an explicit and well-articulated reason to do this. Simpler code also typically runs faster. We just found two complications skulking in the code of this model. One restricts agent movement to an arbitrary distance, 10, from the current location. Why 10 and not 5 or 25? Does this choice make a difference to the model's output? The other prohibits multiple occupancy of residential spaces and variable housing densities. Why? Does this make a difference? We answer both of these questions in a systematic way in Section 4 after we stop treating the model as a discovery tool and start exercising it rigorously using carefully designed suites of computer simulations.

So what makes agents so unhappy that they want to move house? The assumption about this is the core of the Schelling segregation model, implemented in the vital `update-turtles` procedure. This is called first in `setup` and then once every model cycle in `go`. We declared four agent-specific variables at the start of the code, and this procedure updates the values of these variables, every cycle of the model, in light of events that took place during the cycle. This finishes by resetting the crucial `happy?` variable for every agent, which, as we have seen, determines whether or not an agent wants to move. The other three variables are used to determine the value of `happy?`, counting each agent's similar and different neighbors and the resulting total number of neighbors. (In the interests of clarity I deleted the uninteresting visualization code from the bottom of this procedure.)

```
to update-turtles
  ask turtles [
      ;; in next two lines, we use "neighbors" to test the eight patches
      ;; surrounding the current patch
      set similar-nearby count (turtles-on neighbors) with
        [color = [color] of myself]
      set other-nearby count (turtles-on neighbors) with
        [color != [color] of myself]
      set total-nearby similar-nearby + other-nearby
      set happy? similar-nearby >= (%-similar-wanted *
        total-nearby / 100)
      ]
end
```

The procedure asks agents to do several things. The instructions for what to do, as before, are contained between square brackets. Each instruction asks agents to `set` one of their variables, replacing the old value with a new one. The first agent variable updated is `similar-nearby`, which is set to:

```
count (turtles-on neighbors) with [color = [color] of myself]
```

The `count` instruction counts the number of agents conforming to a particular description. In this case the description is `turtles-on neighbors`, the number of turtles on neighboring patches who satisfy (`with`) the condition [color = [color] of myself], in other words, who have the same color as the agent doing the counting. This is more or less self-evident, though the punctuation is important here and is a potential source of error. Round brackets are used in NetLogo when they remove what would otherwise be an ambiguity. We are counting agents on neighboring patches here, not the patches themselves. If we removed the round brackets from turtles-on neighbors with, then the machine would read this as an instruction referring to neighbors with the same color, not (turtles-on neighbors) with the same color. This sort of thing can be tiresome to get right and is a very common source of error. Having executed this instruction, the agents know how many neighboring agents have the same color as themselves.

There is a further potential source of error in the expression myself, which can get confused with another expression, self. Using one expression rather than the other can cause catastrophic errors, and understanding what might go wrong gives us another insight into programming ABMs. In the count expression we just looked at, one agent is counting other agents – those on neighboring patches with the some color. The agent doing the counting, or doing anything else, is myself. When the agent refers to other agents (when counting them, for example), it thinks of these and themselves, or itself. The expression in NetLogo is self, which is definitely confusing. Say you mistakenly wrote the above count expression as:

count (turtles-on neighbors) with [color = [color] of self]

This looks reasonable on the surface and is perfectly valid NetLogo code. (See it in the bad model **Segregation 1.04**.) Worse, it will not crash the model. But the model will now be completely wrong. (Actually, in this case no agent will ever move.) What you've done with the bad code is count neighboring agents with the same color as *themselves*, not as *yourself*, which is stupid. Keep this straight by thinking of *yourself* as myself, the agent taking the action, while *other* agents you are dealing with are "themselves" or "itself" – self for short.

The next update is set other-nearby. This has almost identical code but asks agents to count neighboring agents with a different color from the asking agent. In NetLego, != means "not equal to," so with color != [color] of myself specifies agents with a different color from you. The third update, set total-nearby similar-nearby + other-nearby, speaks for itself, simply adding the totals of similar and different neighboring agents.

Finally, we come to the heart of the matter. What makes agents happy? A single line of code tells us this:

```
set happy? similar-nearby >= (%-similar-wanted * total-nearby / 100)
```

This sets the value of the Boolean variable happy? to either "true" or "false" depending on whether or not the logical condition that follows it is satisfied. In words this condition is that, for the agent in question, the observed number of similar neighboring agents must exceed or equal (written >=) the number the agent wants. If it does, then happy? is true; else happy? is false. The percentage of similar agents wanted is held by the %-similar-wanted global, which, as we have seen, is set by a slider on the interface. So %-similar-wanted / 100 gives the *proportion* of similar neighbors wanted and %-similar-wanted * total-nearby / 100 gives the *number* of similar neighbors wanted, given the total number of neighbors. Fresh out of the box, the default model setting for %-similar-wanted is 30. For agents with a full set of eight neighbors, for example, this means that they are happy? if 30 * 8 / 100 = 2.4 neighbors have the same color. Since agents can have only an integer number of neighbors, this means they are happy if they have three or more similar neighbors out of eight but unhappy if they have two or fewer similar neighbors.

We're nearly done. There's only one more procedure to look at. This is update-globals, which updates the global variables reporting results from the model.

```
to update-globals
    let similar-neighbors sum [similar-nearby] of turtles
    let total-neighbors sum [total-nearby] of turtles
    set percent-similar (similar-neighbors / total-neighbors) * 100
    set percent-unhappy (count turtles with [not happy?] ) / (count turtles) * 100
end
```

There's nothing fancy here but there is one more very useful thing to learn. The third and fourth instructions set two globals, percent-similar and percent-unhappy, in ways that should by now be clear to you. (If not, reread the earlier parts of this section.) The first and second instructions begin with let, and the two variables they refer to, similar-neighbors and total-neighbors, have never been declared and are thus neither global nor agent-specific variables. They've never been mentioned before but they're immediately used in the next line of code. The let instruction is something we use to make our code more elegant and run faster, which is always a good thing. It does this by creating a new *local* variable that only has meaning and existence inside the procedure within which it was created – in this case update-globals. We typically do this to simplify our code when we want to calculate an interim value of something en route to the final calculation in which we are really interested. We don't care about the interim value per se and are happy to throw it away once we have used it. In this case, we have

```
let similar-neighbors sum [similar-nearby] of turtles
```

and

```
let total-neighbors sum [total-nearby] of turtles
```

and we're going to use these two local variables in the instruction that follows:

```
set percent-similar (similar-neighbors / total-neighbors) * 100
```

Doing things this way has two benefits. First, we make the code more legible. We could substitute the expressions giving the values of `similar-neighbors` and `total-neighbors` directly into the code for `set percent-similar`. This would have precisely the same effect but would result in the following uglier and less legible single line of code:

```
set percent-similar (sum [similar-nearby] of turtles /
    sum [total-nearby] of turtles) * 100
```

Using the two local variables has broken this code down into bite-sized chunks, making it both easier to read, easier to debug when there is a problem, and easier to modify going forward. Breaking code down into legible pieces is by far the most important reason to use local variables. We could also declare the two local variables as globals and then change them using `set` rather than `let`. That would also work logically in exactly the same way. But now we're clogging up memory with a global variable that we only use locally in one procedure and giving the machine something else to keep track of.

CODING TIP! LOCAL VARIABLES

Whenever you're specifying and computing a big, ugly expression, it's good coding practice to break this up into a series of simpler expressions using local variables and `let` instructions and then build the expression you want from these parts. This is another example of modularization.

For example, imagine you needed to compute this big, ugly expression in NetLogo:

```
set result (red + 2 * white + 3 * blue + 4 * green) ^ 2 /
    (4 * red + 3 * white + 2 * blue + green) ^ 2
```

("^2" means "squared," or raised to the power of 2)

Breaking this up as follows makes it much nicer, more legible, and easy to change or fix:

```
let hi red + 2 * white + 3 * blue + 4 * green
let lo 4 * red + 3 * white + 2 * blue + green
set result hi ^ 2 / lo ^ 2
```

The Baseline Model Code's Hidden Assumptions

Every model of the real world makes simplifying assumptions. This is what modeling is all about. Some assumptions are clear and explicit. Others are implicit and may be hard to see, even for the model's author. A fundamental principle of good modeling in general and good agent-based modeling in particular is that, as far as possible, your model's assumptions should *not* be left lurking somewhere in the code. They should be standing proudly out there in plain sight, for all to see, to criticize, and to modify. The baseline Schelling segregation model has several substantively important assumptions skulking in its NetLogo code. We make some brief observations about these now, returning to them more rigorously in the next section when we exercise the model in a serious and systematic way.

One question you may well have asked yourself already is whether it is in any way realistic to assume that everyone in the world has precisely the same preference about living with neighbors from different social groups. No, it isn't! This assumption is gross simplification and it's exactly the sort of thing we'll be fixing in Section 4. We'll see this is very easily fixed in the code by declaring %-similar-wanted as an agent-specific, not a global variable, thereby allowing every agent to have different preferences rather than keeping it as a global variable that is constant for all agents and assumes all have the same preferences. It's very common in agent-based modeling to simplify at first, just to get the model running smoothly, by specifying as global variables things that we know very well do vary from agent to agent and then fixing this as we develop the model. When you look at the global variables for any model, you'll often find an implicit assumption that every agent thinks the same way about something, that all agents are clones of each other, when we know that in the real world they might all think differently.

However, fixing this isn't as simple as it might seem. For example, if we specify the variable %-similar-wanted as agent-specific rather than global, then we must now specify precisely *how* this varies from agent to agent. There are going to be many different possible assumptions we can make about this, each potentially with a big impact on our results. So, while we have made our model more realistic, we have also made our lives more difficult. This is an inescapable dilemma for anyone who models anything.

The second observation concerns the fact that every agent has eight, and only eight, possible neighbors. The Moore neighborhoods used by the default model are very small, with the result that there are very few possible states of the world for any agent. We just considered agents who wanted at least 2.4 neighbors to be similar, for example, while the model assumed a maximum of eight neighbors and could give them two or three similar neighbors, never 2.4. This means that, when an agent has eight neighbors, the model will generate exactly the same results for values of `%-similar-wanted` ranging from just over 2/8 (20.1 percent) to 3/8 (37.5 percent) but quite different results for 20.0 or 37.6 `%-similar-wanted`. These sharp discontinuities are major and unrealistic model artifacts arising from using Moore neighborhoods to identify neighbors, and we address this significant problem in Section 4.

A third and final observation concerns another question you might well have asked yourself: only two social groups? of equal size? This is also obviously unrealistic and we return to fix it systematically in Section 4. For now there is a delightfully simple hack with which we can modify the Segregation code to create more social groups. We'll do that right now, since it gives us something interesting to play with. Go to the NetLogo code and find the setup procedure. Find the line of code that says `set color one-of [red green]`. Add a couple of official NetLogo colors to the list: `yellow` and light blue, called `sky` in NetLogo, give a nice contrast on the screen. You now have `set color one-of [red green yellow sky]`, at a stroke creating *four* social groups. (NetLogo colors are described in the NetLogo user manual, which you can access from the "help" menu. Open the user manual, select the programming guide, and scroll down until you find "Colors." You'll find a table with the names of the main colors and a description of how to use much subtler colors than these.)

Hit the check button to make sure you haven't made a mistake. Now go to the interface and hit "setup," then "go." You're in business. Two little words in one line of code change the model in a big way! This is a hack, and in Section 4 we'll use a much more elegant way to change the number of groups without hiding this in the model's code – but it works! Quite often, when we're modifying code to do something new, we'll hack it first to produce the effect we want, and then go back later to write proper code in which everything is much more explicit and well-documented. Leaving undocumented hacks in the code and letting them pile up on top of each other is a great way to generate ugly code that is illegible not only to others but also, most likely, to your own future self. For now, you can save your hack as **Segregation 1.02 four group hack.**

Playing with the Segregation Model

One of the best things about agent-based models is that you can use them to do two quite different things. You can play with them. You can use them as powerful research tools. Playing with your models is both fun and instructive. It can develop your understanding and intuition in creative and powerful but nonetheless enjoyable ways. Using your model as a research tool is serious business. You must think very carefully about what you want to do before you go anywhere near the computer. Having thought this through, you then specify and exercise your model in ways designed to achieve your objectives in a carefully planned and rigorous manner. Well-executed research, including research that uses agent-based models, is extremely satisfying, even if it can't always be described as fun. We'll get serious in the next section, but in the rest of this section we'll play a little with the Segregation model.

Reload the baseline model. Don't change a thing; hit "setup" and "go." You already saw in Figure 2.1 that when the population density is 95 percent and %-similar-wanted is 30 percent, agents move around until they find themselves living in neighborhoods where, on average, about 76 percent of their neighbors belong to the same social group. From the tick counter just above the NetLogo world, you can see that in this run the model took 27 iterations to evolve a pattern of housing segregation where no agent is unhappy, so nobody wants to move.

Now try hitting "setup," but *not* "go," over and over again. You'll keep recreating and rescattering your agents. The four beige monitors and the NetLogo world each time will show a slightly different number of agents with a different scatter of locations and therefore a slightly different average level of unhappiness. Every time you run setup you're triggering random components in your model concerning how agents are assigned to groups and how they scatter around the world. And as we will see throughout the Element, random components such as these are good things, helping us understand and analyze model outputs in rigorous ways. In this example "%-similar" immediately after setup will hop around close to 50 percent. Actually we know *logically* that "%-similar" after setup *must* average 50 percent over many trials. This is because the random allocation of new agents to two equal-sized groups means that, on average, each neighbor of any agent has a 50 percent chance of being from the same group. We don't have to run the model to know that. It's also true, if you look carefully at the logic set out in the model code and care to do the math, that the *average* starting values of each of the other three variables reported can also be calculated precisely.

Now hit "setup" *and* "go" over and over again, looking at the tick counter and "%-similar." You'll see that each simulation always comes to a stop. You'll also see that the number of ticks it takes to do this, "%-similar," and the look of the pattern of segregation that results are all somewhat different each time – but also quite similar. Over and above the random components in the model's setup, there are also random components in every move of every moving agent. These randomly pick the amount each agent spins in place, and the amount it moves forward, having spun. Despite all this random variation, what we see is that over many trials the model does not give us results that are all over the place. Instead, output from multiple run repetitions converges on some particular average value of our key output of interest. For us right now, this is the average percentage of similar neighbors our agents experience after all movement has stopped. We're going to find with a high degree of confidence, when we run the model systematically in the next section, that this average is pretty close to 75 percent similar when our agents want 30 percent of their neighbors to come from the same group.

Now pull the %-similar-wanted slider up to 50 percent. This is in some sense an obvious setting, which says that our agents are unhappy and move home whenever they are from the minority group in their neighborhood. Keep hitting "setup" and "go" and you'll see that the tick counter is typically higher when the model stops. Agents now take longer to find a stable pattern of housing for the obvious reason that their preferences are harder to satisfy. You'll also see that when %-similar-wanted is 50 percent, the %-similar that typically evolves is about 86 percent. Once more, this is *much* more housing segregation than our agents want.

Now we're going to do something that has been done by very few people before. Pull the "%-similar-wanted" slider up to 75 percent. Think about this before hitting "setup" and "go." These agent preferences are going to be very hard to satisfy. When all eight neighboring patches are occupied, it means that neighbors on six out of these must come from the same group. With seven neighboring patches occupied, only six out of seven will make the agent happy, and so on. These constraints are easy enough to satisfy in small local areas but not at all easy *for every agent everywhere in the world* when there are equal numbers of red and blue agents. So hit "setup" and "go," watch the screen, and be patient. You'll see something interesting. The world fairly quickly evolves into a configuration in which nearly all of the agents are living in one or two totally segregated neighborhoods, separated by bands of black empty patches. The only movement happens at the boundaries between these two neighborhoods, where there is a constant churn of unhappy agents. You might think that this in itself gives a good intuition about the real world. You might also think, when looking at the plots as the run keeps going, that the pattern of housing segregation is *never* going to stabilize, that the NetLogo world had converged

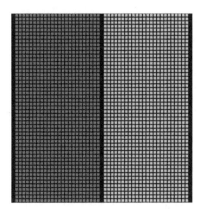

Figure 2.5 Stable configuration of agent positions for any `%-similar-wanted`

on what we can think of as a stochastic steady state in which agents keep moving but the result stays more or less the same. "Number-unhappy" seems to be continuously varying around a constant low mean but never dropping to zero and stopping the run.

You might think that, but you'd be wrong. If you run the model long enough – this will take patience unless you're running it on a supercomputer, and I don't think you are – your agents will typically find a (very rare) configuration of positions that does indeed satisfy the constraints required to make them all happy. So be very careful about assuming, just from looking at everything churning on the screen, that your model will never converge on a stable outcome.

In this example, if we think carefully about this, we can see there are indeed possible configurations of agent locations that satisfy all constraints. One of these (and there may be more, but we only need to identify one possibility) sorts the agents from the two groups into two regions, each completely homogenous socially, with bands of unoccupied patches between regions. If our random scatter just happened to throw the agents into such a configuration, and this is logically possible even if monumentally unlikely, then all our agents would be `happy?` and none would move. Figure 2.5 shows the result of editing the setup code in the NetLogo Segregation model to scatter our agents at the outset in precisely this configuration.

We do this by asking all the left-hand patches to sprout a red agent, all the right-hand patches to sprout a green agent, and not asking the center and edge patches to sprout any agent, as in the model **Segregation 1.03** always stable:

```
ask patches [
    if pxcor <= -1 and pxcor > min-pxcor [sprout 1 [set color red]]
    if pxcor >= 1 and pxcor < max-pxcor [sprout 1 [set color green]]]
```

No matter how high we set %-similar-wanted (no matter how preju-diced we make our agents), they are all happy? and none want to move if they find themselves in the configuration shown in Figure 2.5. Over the very long run – perhaps longer than your lifetime, even if you're using a supercomputer – agents making random movements will eventually find rare stationary states such as this in which they are all happy. We see an example of this in Figure 2.6, which shows an evolved stationary configuration of agent locations when %-similar-wanted is set in the baseline Segregation model to 75.

The model took 9,841 cycles to converge as opposed to at most a couple of dozen with previous settings. You see from the plots that outputs of interest spent most of this time flatlining around a very small number of unhappy agents but not converging to zero. If you were impatient and had not thought things through as we just did, you might have thought the model was never going to converge on a stationary state and stopped it yourself. But the model finally did converge and, as the NetLogo world shows, our agents finally found a configuration of locations

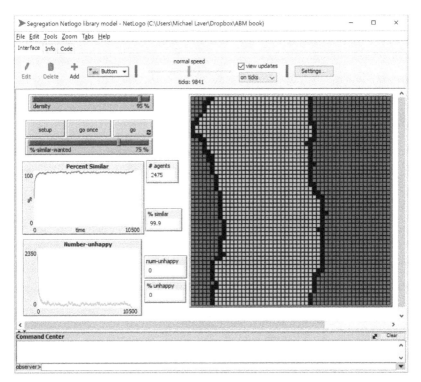

Figure 2.6 Evolved stationary state when %-similar-wanted = 75

very close to the one we just described. But the resemblance is not an exact one. Look at the very bottom left of the world and you'll see a red and a green agent touching corners, without black empty space between them. However, you can quickly satisfy yourself that the "75 percent similar" constraint is satisfied for both of them.

The long time it took this run to converge suggests another trick of the trade. Look at the speed slider above the world. Slide the speed as far to the right as it will go, to the fastest possible setting. The tick counter will speed up and the model will run faster. The price you will pay is that the screen updates will become rather jerky. The *computer itself* is not running any faster; it's already working to finish the job for you as fast as possible. When you drag the NetLogo speed slider to the right, you stop updating the screen with every model tick and do this only once in a while. The *model code* now runs faster because updating the screen takes time, and updating it continuously takes a lot of time. When we start serious work in the next section, we'll want our models to run blindingly fast so that we can do as many runs as possible in any given time. One way we will achieve this is to turn off all screen updates, which will give us a serious speed boost. There will be nothing to look at while the model is running, but we won't care about that because we won't be looking at the screen; rather we will be somewhere else, refreshing ourselves with a nice cup of tea, while the computer does its work.

Now for something completely different. Go back to the `%-similar-wanted` slider and pull it up a tiny notch to 76 percent. Hit `setup` and `go`. The NetLogo world suddenly seems to have flipped into a chaotic state. Most agents are churning locations without any apparent improvement in their happiness. This is not something that has been noticed by people writing about the Schelling model and is a great benefit of having a computer model to play with vigorously until we break something. As we will see throughout this Element, breaking models and then finding out why they broke is one of the main things we are trying to do when running ABMs on the computer. In contrast to the real world, when we break a computational model and then fix it, we nearly always make it stronger. When we get serious about computational modeling, we always try to break the model!

In this case, when we look at the screen while the model runs, it really does seem as if the model will never converge. The reason is that with 76 `%-similar-wanted`, if all neighboring squares are occupied, then six out of eight neighbors from the same group is no longer good enough. The tiny shift from 75 to 76 percent makes a big difference, exposing a sharp discontinuity in how the model works. More important in this particular case, with only four neighboring squares occupied (as often happens at the boundary between

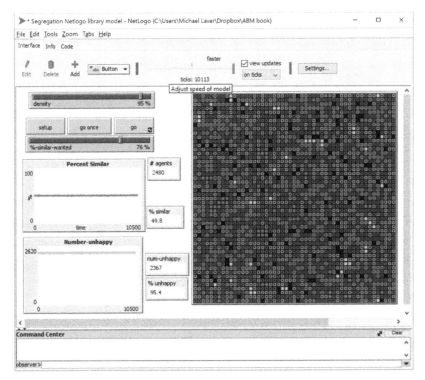

Figure 2.7 Chaotic state when %-similar-wanted = 76

regions), having three out of four neighbors the same is suddenly no longer good enough. Go back to the far bottom left of the world in Figure 2.6. The red square touching the green at its corner has four neighboring patches occupied, three of which are red. This satisfies a 75 %-similar-wanted constraint but not a 76 %-similar-wanted constraint. The configuration of agent positions in Figure 2.6 would no longer be stable, since that red agent will move. Making constraints more severe means that finding a stable configuration of agent locations becomes even more difficult. However, we have already seen logically that, given an *extremely* long sequence of random agent moves, a stable configuration is still logically possible.

Figure 2.7 shows a screenshot of a model run after more than 10,000 cycles, showing that agents were no closer to converging on a stable configuration of locations than they were at the very beginning of the run. Not only that but almost every agent is unhappy. We might take from this the substantive intuition that, when prejudice against other groups is very high, it may be almost impossible to find a configuration of locations that makes everyone happy – that our agents are simply too prejudiced ever to be happy. For them all to be happy is almost, but not absolutely, impossible. Go back to the logical possibility shown in Figure 2.5, with all agents in two completely homogenous regions and pure black unoccupied space between them. This must now be perfectly achieved, not "sort of" achieved as in Figure 2.6. Logically, however, if agents keep moving randomly until they are all `happy?`, no matter how long this takes, then this will eventually happen. In practice, it may take a very long time for this to happen, maybe so long that you or your computer will wear out before it happens. I have never myself with my own two eyes seen this version of the model converge with `%-similar-wanted` set to 76. However tempted I might be to say on this basis that the model will never converge, I know logically from Figure 2.5 that convergence is indeed possible over the extremely long run. If I throw a pair of dice enough times, I will eventually throw the million double-sixes in a row that allows the model to converge. You might think intuitively that this will never happen. But you know logically that it is *possible* even if extraordinarily *improbable*. Over an evolutionary time-scale it will eventually happen.

There are two important lessons here. First, there is no substitute for thinking though the logical implications of your model. In this example we don't have to sit around forever watching the screen and wondering if the model will eventually converge on a stable configuration of agent locations; we know logically that it will eventually converge. Second, we may conclude, if we do run the model, that it takes so very long to converge that satisfying our agents' preferences is *to all intents and purposes* impossible. What we are then saying is that we're going to treat agent preferences as *effectively* impossible to satisfy in these circumstances if the only way to satisfy them is to throw a million double-sixes in a row. We don't say the model will *never* converge on a stable config-uration of agent locations, but for practical purposes we treat the model *as if* it will never converge with this parameterization.

You can also play with the `density` slider and find out how that works, but right now we want to play with that nice little four-group model we hacked a while back. Recall, we did this by editing one line of the setup procedure code to:

```
set color one-of [red green yellow sky]
```

Either load the file you saved with this (**Segregation 1.02 four group hack**) or make the edit now. Hit `setup` and `go`. With the default setting of 30 for `%-similar-wanted` you'll see that agents quickly find a configuration of locations that makes them all happy. Do this over and over and you'll notice a couple of things. First, the model takes longer to converge on stable agent locations with four groups than with two – it's a harder problem to solve. Second, when things do converge, this tends to result in about 71 or

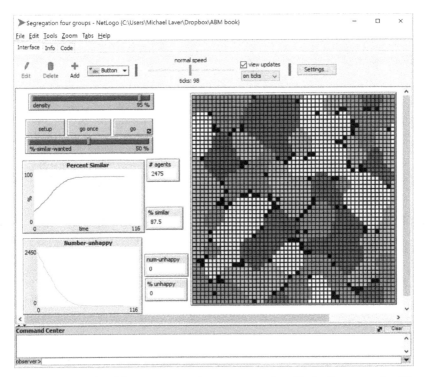

Figure 2.8 Evolved four-group stationary state when %-similar-wanted = 50

72 percent of agents having similar neighbors, as opposed to about 74 or 75 percent when agents wanted 30 percent of their neighbors to be similar. This is a small but significant difference. So does having more social groups lead to less social segregation? Not necessarily, as we'll now find out.

Drag %-similar-wanted up to 50. We're now in a world where agents move if they find themselves in a minority. Keep hitting setup and go. Figure 2.8 shows what you might find. Things do tend to converge quite quickly, leaving agents with about 87 or 88 percent of neighbors from the same group. This is a tad *higher* than the 86 percent or so we found with only two social groups, though we'll need to do more systematic work to confirm this with any real confidence. What we are seeing here is that the relationship between %-similar-wanted and evolved percent-similar *depends on the number of different social groups*. This is the sort of *interaction* effect we very often find when we model social behavior.

Here is something else quite striking. Move %-similar-wanted up a notch to 51. Hit setup and run. Chaos! Figure 2.9 shows output from a run in which the model was stopped after over 22,500 cycles. Agents had come no closer to converging on a stable configuration of locations and most of them were unhappy.

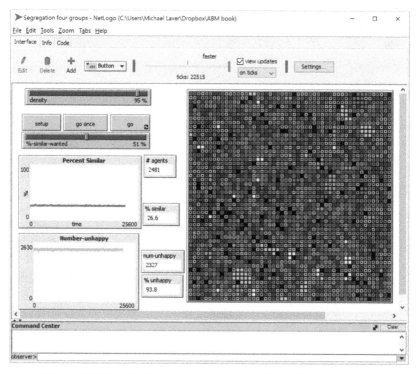

Figure 2.9 Chaotic four-group state when %-similar-wanted = 51

This is similar to what happened in the baseline model with two social groups when we went from 75 to 76 %-similar-wanted. Given the eight-cell Moore neighborhood that is determining our agents' happiness, the shift to 76 %-similar-wanted with two groups triggered new constraints that are very hard, though not logically impossible given an infinite amount of time, to satisfy. Computationally, we hit a wall. The same thing happens with four social groups, but in this case we hit the computational wall when we go past 50 %-similar-wanted. Adding more groups has a major impact on constraints that, given eight cell Moore neighborhoods, makes it very hard to satisfy all agent preferences. This is almost certainly the main effect of adding more groups to the Schelling segregation model and is something previous authors who have written on this model have not noticed. We turn in what follows to investigate in a systematic way the important question of whether this is a general finding or simply a model artifact of using eight-cell Moore neighborhoods rather than a more realistic specification of social neighborhoods. Cue the next section!

3 Social Segregation: Power User

We've so far been *playing* with the Schelling Segregation model as implemented in the NetLogo models library. We kept hitting `setup` and `go`, watching the model run, and looking at the state of the world after all agents had converged on a stable pattern of housing locations that made each of them happy. Running the out-of-the-box NetLogo segregation model with its default settings, `%-similar-wanted` at 30 percent and `density` at 95 percent, we typically arrived at an outcome where about 75 percent of our agents found themselves with neighbors from the same social group. This is fine to get a sense of things, but it's not a solid *finding* we can reasonably expect others to take seriously. The way to think about this is to ask if anyone else anywhere in the world, using any machine, can take your code, run it themselves, and find the same thing. If this is true, then your finding is worth reporting and worth others taking seriously. This is not unlike rolling a dice to find out what's on each of the sides. If we roll it twice and both times come up with a six, we're hardly going to tell the world that every side is a six. But if we roll it a million times and every time it comes up six, then we'd probably bet the farm that every side is a six, and that the next roll also will come up six. There's still an infinitesimally small probability that this is a regular dice and we just happened to throw a million sixes in a row. But we would be absolutely right to infer that this is *almost certainly* not true.

From now on we stop playing with the model and become power users. We do this by running the Segregation model over and over again, recording the results of each run in a systematic way and summarizing our results. We run the model enough times to make us confident that anyone else running the same model in the same way will get the same results. We do this using a powerful feature of NetLogo called Behavior Space, which allows you to exercise models in a systematic way using suites of computational experiments. Again, we learn by doing and jump right into our first experiment. This is designed to estimate, if we run the model with its out-of-the-box default settings until all agents are happy?, the average percentage of similar neighbors (level of social segregation) for the whole population of agents. When we played casually with the model, this number looked to be about 75 percent. But what is our *rigorous* estimate of this? To answer this question, we run the default model 1,000 times with the same settings until each run reaches a stationary state and record the results of each run. We then calculate the average of evolved `percent-similar` for all runs as well as the amount of variation around this average. Fortunately this takes almost no time in NetLogo and the results will be a lot more impressive than just hitting `setup` and `go` a bunch of times and guessing or even calculating the average.

Designing and Running Computational Experiments

Fire up the baseline Segregation model from the NetLogo library. Don't hit setup but go to the tools menu and select "BehaviorSpace." You see a little pop-up screen in which you should click "new." This will give you the main Behavior Space design window, which you use to specify your experiments. Figure 3.1 shows an example. You're going to spend a *lot* of time with Behavior Space, which will become one of your best friends, so you need to get *very* familiar with it

As you become a power user you'll use this screen time and time again. There's a lot to it, and we're eager to dive right in and run our first experiment, so we'll just look at parts of the window for now. Pass over the "vary variables" pane at the top. This is very important, but we're not yet going to vary anything,

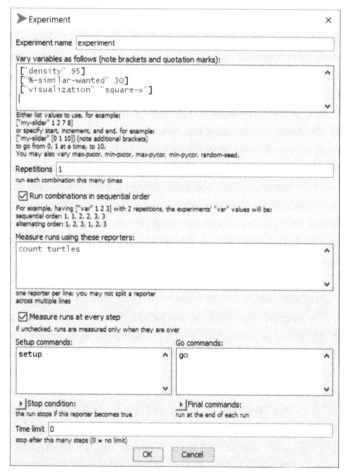

Figure 3.1 Default Behavior Space design window for the Segregation model

just keep rerunning the model with its default settings. Next you come to "Repetitions." This tells Behavior Space how many times to repeat the model run for a given combination of variable settings. We want to repeat the same model run enough times that we are confident in our findings. But we don't want to run it too many times because, once we are confident in our findings, we're eager to get on to the next challenge and don't want to waste time having the computer tell us something we already know. This is all about the efficient budgeting of computer time, an important matter to which we return several times in what follows. For now we note that the only damage caused by doing too much computing is wasting time whereas, if you do too little computing, you can't rely on your findings. If in doubt, therefore, err on the side of over-computing. We'll be systematic about this later and take nothing for granted; but, to get things going, rely on the fact that 1,000 repetitions of a model run has emerged in the agent-based modeling community as a reasonable rule of thumb for a job such as this. So type 1000 into this box.

The next pane you come to is "Measure runs using these reporters," which tells Behavior Space what you want to measure and record. This defaults to `count turtles`, which will count the number of agents created at the start of each run, a crushingly boring quantity of no interest whatsoever. Delete this and replace it with what does interest you, which is `percent-similar`.

Next, you see a check box with "Measure runs at every step." If this box is checked, this process will record values of `percent-similar` every cycle of every repetition of the model, not just at the end of each run after every agent is `happy?`. These values measure transient states of the model en route to the final state. The transient states are sometimes of great interest, but right now we care only about the final stable configurations of agents' positions, not about how our agents got there. Uncheck this box to spare yourself from a huge amount of uninteresting output.

Next, you see panes with instructions telling Behavior Space which commands to use for setup and go. In this case these are just the model's `setup` and `go` procedures, so the default settings are fine. Down the line we'll see how we might want to get fancier with these.

Finally, you come to a pane asking for a "Time limit." This is the number of cycles Behavior Space will let the model run before stopping and recording results. The default is "0", which means the model run goes on forever unless it stops itself. Recall that the NetLogo Segregation model code has a line that does stop itself when all agents are `happy?`. But also recall we found model settings that can cause the model to run for a very long time indeed. Indeed, while you may not have found this yet, on rare occasions the model can run for an extraordinarily long time even with the default settings. So backstop the model's self-stopping code by entering 1000 for the "Time limit." Most run repetitions stop long before that, but we want to catch those rare ones when the model seems to run forever, causing our experiment to go on and on without stopping.

I'm using an important terminological convention here, which is not universal but which I find helpful when designing and analyzing computational experiments. I talk of a model run as a particular parameterization of the model, in this case a particular set of values for key model variables (parameters) in the Behavior Space design window. Here we specify a single model run. I talk of a run repetition or repetition as a repetition of the same run with the same parameter setting but with a different random seed. Here we specify 1,000 repetitions of one model run. I talk of an iteration (or cycle) of the model as a single iteration of the model's code within a particular run repetition. Here we limit each run repetition to 1,000 iterations, steps in NetLogo. NetLogo logs the number of steps after a new `setup` in its internal `tick` variable. Others, including sometimes even NetLogo, use the terms run and repetition more casually, but I suggest you stick to the convention I set out here to keep both your thinking and your writing as precise as possible.

We've designed the experiment and need to give it a name, let's say "experiment 1" for now. Naming experiments in an informative way is *extremely* important. At the end of this experiment, save the NetLogo model under a different name (such as **Segregation 1.10**) and this will save your design for experiment 1. The key thing about *any* experiment, computational or otherwise, is that you and anyone else in the world must be able to repeat it, doing *exactly* what you did before. *That's why you must carefully name and save every experiment you do in NetLogo.* You might think you'll always remember what you did, but I guarantee you won't. You need to record and save this, not least so you can show others *precisely* what you did, so they can do precisely the same thing and check your results. At the end of all this, your Behavior Space design screen will look like the one in Figure 3.2.

Click OK and you'll get back to the run screen shown in the top panel of Figure 3.3, which now highlights the name of your newly designed experiment. When you've designed several experiments for the same model, which will happen soon, you'll see each of them listed and can highlight the one you want to run. Hit "run" and you'll see the "Run options" screen shown in the bottom panel of Figure 3.3. Check only the option "table output" if it's not already selected – this is much the easiest to work with. The code will also count the number of virtual cores your machine can use for this, defaulting to running parallel repetitions of your model on each core. "Simultaneous runs in parallel"

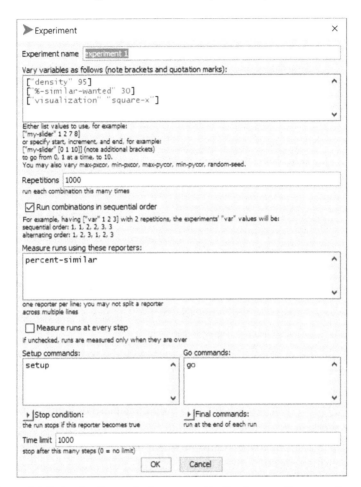

Figure 3.2 Behavior Space design screen for the Segregation experiment 1

in the "Run options" screen tells us that you're running on an eight-core machine and that the code will not stupidly run 1,000 repetitions of your model, one after the other, but will cleverly run eight repetitions at the same time. This hugely reduces the time you wait for your results, so do not change this setting.

Click OK and you'll be asked what you want to call the results file and where you want to save this file in a screen that looks like the one in the top panel of Figure 3.4 – this is the screen generated for Windows 10 but others will look very similar. Even though you're eager to set the machine spinning, stay focused and be very careful to give the output file a name that will mean something to you when you come back to it, and to save it in a place where you'll be able to find it months or even years later. Beware of default names offered to you and be

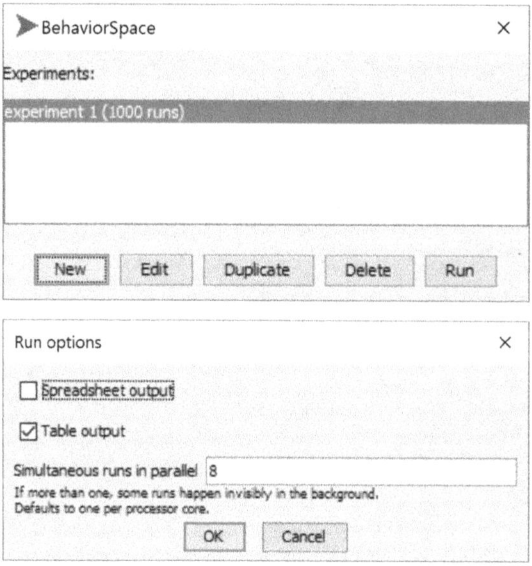

Figure 3.3 Behavior Space run screens for Segregation experiment 1

very careful not to overwrite your old work with the results you're about to generate. This may all sound obvious but, believe me, it's easy to forget.

Once you hit "Save" the simulation will start running and you'll see the "Running Experiment" screen shown in the bottom panel of Figure 3.4. You've still got work to do because you should now uncheck "Update view" and "Update plots and monitors," both of which are checked by default. As we discussed earlier, this will speed up your runs because it stops time-consuming updates of the screen, which are rarely helpful when running the model 1,000 times. The "Running Experiment" screen updates you on the progress of your experiment. You get a good sense of how long you have to wait by seeing how many runs have completed and how long these took. In this case 68 runs took 4 seconds, so 680 might take about 40 seconds and the full 1,000 runs should take about a minute. When this screen disappears, the experiment has finished running and you can look at your results. These are stored in the file and location you specified and you can now load the results file into a spreadsheet program (it's in .csv format).

Staying true to the maxim that if you have access to a computer you needn't spend a single penny on this, I use the free software Google Sheets in what follows. (You also can use your preferred spreadsheet or data analysis software to analyze your results.) The file your experiment just generated is 1,007 rows long and six columns wide. You may need more powerful analysis software for more ambitious experiments, since it's easy to generate output files with

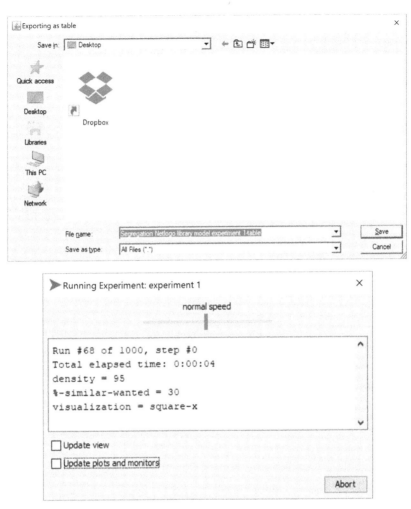

Figure 3.4 Behavior Space file save and update screens for Segregation experiment 1

millions of rows. For now Google Sheets will get us most places we want to go in fine style. The top and bottom panels of Table 3.1 show the top and bottom few rows of this data file, loaded into Google Sheets. You do this by firing up Google Sheets, choosing "import" under the file menu, choosing "Upload" in the "Import file" window, then dragging your results file into the resulting pane.

The top six rows record important information about the run. What was the version of NetLogo you used? What NetLogo model and experiment did you run? When did you run it and what was the size of the NetLogo world you ran it on? Row 7 names the variables whose values for each run repetition you find in the next 1,000 rows. If you load your results into data analysis software, you can

Table 3.1 Top and bottom rows of 1,007-row results file for Segregation experiment 1

BehaviorSpace results (NetLogo 6.0.1)
Segregation Netlogo library model.nlogo
experiment 1

08/07/2017 17:52:00:690 +0100

min-pxcor	max-pxcor	min-pycor	max-pycor			
−25	25	−25	25			
[run number]	density	%-similar-wanted	visualization	[step]	percent-similar	
5	95	30	"square-x"	14	76.23657058	
6	95	30	"square-x"	15	74.78910838	
7	95	30	"square-x"	16	74.53330505	
3	95	30	"square-x"	16	75.2145107	
			. . .			
996	95	30	"square-x"	18	74.03563941	
999	95	30	"square-x"	14	75.3027406	
1000	95	30	"square-x"	13	74.53623814	
986	95	30	"square-x"	1000	73.32133023	
Average					74.9	
Standard deviation					1.09	

usually use these variable names directly. The first five columns of data record, first, the run repetition number (in the order repetitions were completed on the eight cores of the machine, so not in sequence), then in the next three columns the default settings of the key global variables, which you did not vary in this experiment. The fifth column, "[step]," gives the run cycle associated with the observation, which in this case is interesting because it records the number of cycles before the model stopped. Finally, you find the values of the output variable(s) you asked for, in this case `percent-similar`.

If you use other software to analyze these data, you'll likely want to delete the top six rows and use the seventh row for variable names. First, *save the edited version of your output file under a different name* and store the original file generated by NetLogo in a safe place. Then, no matter what mistakes you make, you can always go back to the original, which also stores key information about the experiment in the first six rows.

For now we use Google Sheets to get what we want, which is the average evolved `percent-similar` across all 1,000 run repetitions and the amount of variation around this, measured using the standard deviation. The 1,000 values of `percent-similar` are stored in cells F8–F1007 of the spreadsheet, so typing "=average(F8:F1007)" into a blank cell gives us the average of these, while "=STDEV(F8:F1007)" gives the standard deviation. Put these summaries under the column they refer to, as in the bottom panel of Table 3.1. Our best estimate of the average `percent-similar` is 74.9 percent with a standard deviation of 1.09. We therefore expect about 95 percent of our observations to lie within two standard deviations on either side of the average in the range of 72.7–77.1 percent. We expect to get similar values of these two estimates each time we rerun this experiment. We can therefore treat these estimates as findings from the model, which we are comfortable reporting to the rest of the world.

Both the average and the variation in `percent-similar` are substantively important. This is because there is fundamental variation in the percentage of similar neighbors arising from the Schelling segregation model, variation we also expect to find in the real world. This is quite different from the problem we face when, for example, we measure the weight of a sack of potatoes using a number of different scales, none perfectly accurate. In that case we think there is a single true weight of the sack of potatoes. If we measure this weight with five different scales, each with some random error, we're more confident in the average weight returned by the five scales than in the weight of any one scale. If we had 1,000 unbiased but error-prone scales, we would be very confident indeed about the average of the 1,000 different weights returned. We could measure our confidence using the standard error of our estimated average. The standard error shrinks, the more unbiased observations we collect. This is not, however, our problem here and is not the problem we generally face in agent-based modeling. We think of the outcomes of each model run as possible states of a real world that are indeed different, while at the same time sharing similarities, just as we do not expect the real world always to end up in exactly the same state from exactly the same starting point. We are therefore *very* interested in the level of variation to expect in possible states of the world – in fundamental variation in this sense. Because we do not think there is some underlying true state of the world we are trying inaccurately to discover, we measure variation using standard deviations, not standard errors.

There is, however, an important and fairly common wrinkle in these results, which you can see in the bottom data row in Table 3.1. This shows that repetition 986 ran to 1,000 steps but was stopped, short of convergence, by code we added to stop run repetitions after 1,000 iterations. The value of `percent-similar` recorded for this repetition, which you can see is lower than others, does not reflect a stable configuration in which all agents are `happy?`. This is not the only time a repetition terminated short of convergence

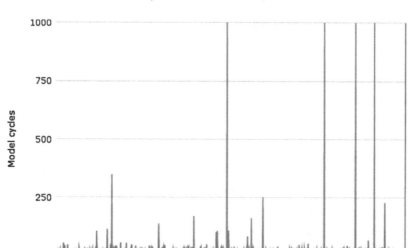

Figure 3.5 Model cycles needed to complete each of 1,000 repetitions in experiment 1

in the 1,000-run experiment. Figure 3.5 diagnoses the extent of this problem, showing a bar plot of the number of steps – model cycles – each of the 1,000 repetitions took to complete. We see that five of the 1,000 repetitions artificially terminated at 1,000 cycles rather than stopping because all agents had converged on a stable location. A few other repetitions lasted much longer than the others but did stop with every agent happy.

What should we do about this? One answer is not to stop repetitions when they hit a predetermined number of cycles, letting each continue to completion. But this might have caused this particular experiment to run for hours, even days, rather than for just one minute. We could delete the five artificially terminated repetitions. This throws away information and risks biasing our results, but in an unknown way, since we've no idea whether deleted repetitions would have terminated with systematically higher, or lower, values of per-cent-similar. We can leave them in peace and reckon that five slightly "off" results out of 1,000 won't do too much violence to our estimate.

Note that a more robust measure of the typical model output, such as the median, does not help us here. This is because we have no way of knowing whether artificially terminated repetitions, if allowed to continue to convergence, would have systematically resulted in output values at the high or low end of the 1,000 observations. We do know they are atypical, having taken so long to converge. The important thing is to be aware of, and explicit about what you are doing. The bottom line, however, is that if you find a substantial number of artificially terminated repetitions, then you are terminating them too soon and just have to accept that you need to let repetitions run longer and devote more time to this experiment.

Manipulating Model Parameters

We just conducted 1,000 run repetitions to generate a reliable estimate of the average and standard deviation of evolved social segregation, measured by `percent-similar`, for out-of-the-box model settings. This is an important *technical* accomplishment but is not *substantively* very interesting in itself. What really interests us is how key model outputs, such as evolved `percent-similar`, are affected by *changes* in key model inputs, such as `%-similar-wanted`. We played with this in Section 2 but now want to investigate it systematically. BehaviorSpace is designed to help you do this. So let's select BehaviorSpace again from the Tools menu and design another experiment. You can duplicate and edit your existing experiment to save time but be sure to give it a new name! We want to vary model parameters, so we're going to use the "Vary variables" pane at the top of the design window. Delete the boring `["visualization" "square-x"]` variable, since you're never going to use it and it only clogs things up. Leave `density` as it is for now. We want to vary `%-similar-wanted` in a systematic way. For the moment let's investigate effects of five different values of this, say, 20, 30, 40, 50, and 60. As a practical matter we don't explore higher settings than this, because we already know from playing with the model that, even when `%-similar-wanted` is set to 60, we're already hitting 98 or 99 percent evolved `percent-similar`, leaving very little upside in our output quantity of interest.

We therefore specify `["%-similar-wanted" 20 30 40 50 60]`. This specifies five model runs, telling NetLogo to run the model many times for each of the five specified settings of `%-similar-wanted`. You specify the number of repetitions of each run in the "Repetitions" pane below. If you specify 250 repetitions for each of the five runs, for example, you specify 1250 run repetitions. If you find you need more repetitions for a bulletproof estimate of your quantities of interest, then you can do more repetitions later, even overnight if you like. *But it's a good idea to sketch potentially interesting results first to make sure you've specified things correctly.* You don't want to launch a monster experiment only to find out many hours later that you made a silly mistake and have to redo everything. Since we found that a few run repetitions were not completing even with the default settings, let's increase the time limit from 1,000 to 2,000 iterations.

Again, see this as a sketch of potential results. If you find you need a much longer time limit – and you might, since you're investigating much higher values of `%-similar-wanted` than before – then you can conduct a much

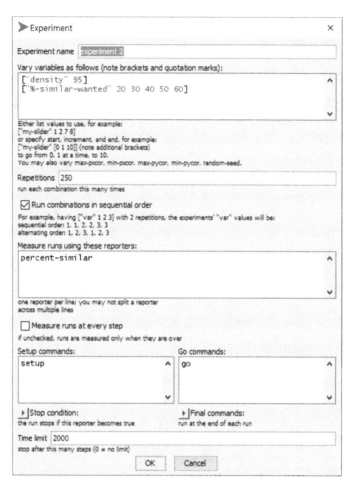

Figure 3.6 Behavior Space design screen for the Segregation experiment 2

longer and more bulletproof experiment later. The net result is the BehaviorSpace design window shown in Figure 3.6. First, save this as experiment 2 in the model **Segregation 1.10**. Now run your experiment and see the results! It will take a *lot* longer to run than the previous experiment, since runs with higher values of %-similar-wanted take a long time to complete.

After the first six lines of header information the business end of your output spreadsheet from this run should look something like, but not exactly like Table 3.2.

The %-similar-wanted column shows that BehaviorSpace started the experiment by setting this global variable to 20. If you scroll down the file, you'll see 250-repetition batches of results, each batch increasing the setting for %-similar-wanted in increments of 10, as requested, until this reaches the highest requested setting of 60. We're interested in the relationship between %-

Table 3.2 Top rows of 1250-row results file for Segregation experiment 2

[run number]	density	%-similar-wanted	[step]	percent-similar
			8	
6	95	20	7	56.43184483
4	95	20	8	54.15345593
8	95	20	9	54.24018822
7	95	20	8	55.36091178

similar-wanted and the values of evolved percent-similar, when all agents have stopped moving and are happy?. *The easiest and most intuitive way to see this is to plot corresponding values of these two variables against each other* for each of the 1250 run repetitions of the experiment. You can do this very easily in Google Sheets by highlighting the two columns of data and asking for a scatterplot. (Access scatterplots via the "insert chart" symbol on the Google Sheets toolbar.)

When edited a little to clean it up and make labels more informative, your plot will look like the one shown in Figure 3.7. For each of the five investigated values of %-similar-wanted this plots with an "x" the 250 different values of evolved percent-similar after each run stopped. These are so tightly clustered you can barely see just a few of the individual plot marks; what you see are five black bands that contain all of the simulation results. This tells us right away that for a given value of %-similar-wanted there was some variation, but not much, in the percentage of similar neighbors that agents experienced after they were all happy? and stopped moving. We see an increasing nonlinear relationship between rising values of %-similar-wanted and rising levels of evolved social segregation. We say the relationship between these two variables is nonlinear because it's not possible to draw a single straight line summarizing all the various clusters of points in the plot. Many interesting social relationships are nonlinear, so we're not surprised by this. Finally, we see that, once %-similar-wanted reaches 60 percent, levels of evolved social segregation max out close to 100 percent. Increasing %-similar-wanted beyond 60 percent cannot result in higher levels of social segregation, since we are already close to 100 percent.

One thing we saw when playing with the model in the last section was that it became much harder for agents to find configurations of locations that make them all happy? when they want a higher proportion of their neighbors to come from the same group as themselves – when we increase %-similar-wanted. Given the eight-cell Moore neighborhoods to which agents are

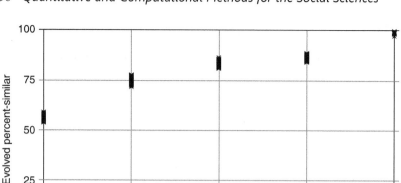

Figure 3.7 Relationship between %-similar-wanted and evolved percent-similar, density = 95

programmed to pay attention, increasing %-similar-wanted progressively adds more constraints to configurations of agent locations that make all agents happy. This makes it progressively harder for agents to find a configuration that satisfies all constraints. We also saw that we seem to hit a computational wall in this search when the density of agents is 95 percent, as %-similar-wanted goes past 60 percent, and particularly past 75 percent, after which the model takes an extraordinarily long time to converge.

We see this more systematically with another scatterplot using the results from our most recent experiment. Figure 3.8 plots the relationship between %-similar-wanted and the number of model cycles it takes to make all agents happy?. The results are striking. The model quickly converges on stable configurations of happy? agents when %-similar-wanted is 50 percent or less. But when this variable is increased to 60 percent, we start to see the computational wall, with the model taking *very* much longer to converge, and sometimes not converging by the time 2,000 cycles have been reached and the repetition is artificially stopped. This is useful to know. Figure 3.7 tells us we're not going to get more juice out of the model with these settings when %-similar-wanted goes past 60 percent. Figure 3.8 tells us that when %-similar-wanted goes past 60 percent, we hit a computational wall of pain. This gives us two good reasons not to set %-similar-wanted over 60, since doing so generates a huge computational load but yields uninteresting results.

This is an important general lesson in how to budget your resources when designing computational experiments. Your computer, no matter how snazzy, has

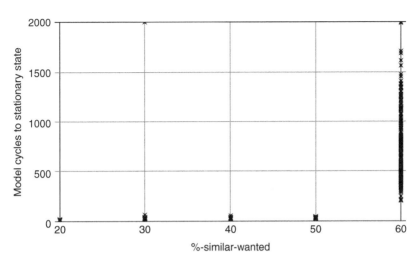

Figure 3.8 Relationship between %-similar-wanted and model cycles to stationary state: density = 95

a finite amount of computing power. You, your own self, have a finite amount of available time. These limits combine to set your computational budget. You want to spend this budget as efficiently as possible. You might without thinking too carefully simply specify a wide range of parameter values, in this case perhaps the logically possible range of 0–100 in increments, say, of 10. As we just saw, however, not all parameterizations of the model are equally informative. Outputs may, for example, be approaching a logical upper bound with no logical reason for them to decline. Here segregation levels closely approach 100 percent once %-similar-wanted is 60. We know logically that this key output will continue to creep even closer to 100 as we increase this key input parameter, but this is of little substantive interest. Runs with %-similar-wanted over 60 are *extremely* expensive, furthermore, and blow our computational budget. So there is a double reason not to do them. There is no hard-and-fast rule here, only common sense informed by logic. Once outputs are converging on some logical bound and/or when run repetitions start eating deeply into your finite computational budget, you need to think carefully about whether you really need to investigate the model parameterizations involved. If you had an infinitely powerful computer you'd never need to worry about this. But you don't, so you do.

Monte Carlo Experiments

Figure 3.7 and 3.8 show effects of just a few values of %-similar-wanted. This is because we conducted a *grid sweep* of the effects of %-similar-wanted, investigating particular values of this parameter chosen at regularly spaced intervals. We did so because this is how BehaviorSpace is set up, but it's not necessarily the best way to do things. We don't really care, for example, about what happens when %-similar-wanted is *precisely* 30 percent. What we care about is how evolved percent-similar responds to variations in %-similar-wanted. *Why repeat a model run hundreds of times for a precise parameter setting we don't care about*? Why not continuously vary model parameters within ranges that interest us? It's actually very easy to do this by making BehaviorSpace choose values for key parameters randomly within specified ranges. This is a *Monte Carlo* model parametrization.

While grid sweeps are common in published ABM results and are the default experimental design in NetLogo, they're not always the best way to do things. Monte Carlo model parameterization can be better and more general. You very often want to investigate the effects, not of some *particular* value of a parameter, but of *changes* in this. In this situation, Monte Carlo parametrization may be more appropriate. We specify this in BehaviorSpace with a simple fix to default setup commands to give a design window like the one in Figure 3.9. This is experiment 3 in the model **Segregation 1.10**. First, you see we left only ["density" 90] in the "Vary variables . . ." pane, lowering the value of this parameter a little to allow the model to converge more quickly without, as we'll shortly see, any substantial effect on results. Go down to the "Setup commands" pane and you'll see that this is now where we're setting the %-similar-wanted parameter, in a line of code *after* the main setup procedure. The full code, sadly, is hidden in this window, but it reads as follows:

```
setup
set %-similar-wanted 20 + random-float 40
```

What this does is tell BehaviorSpace to *first* execute the setup procedure, which will read the value of %-similar-wanted from the interface. *Having done this, reset* %-similar-wanted to a number that is 20 plus a random number drawn from the range 0–40, that is, to a random number in the range 20–60, which is what we want to do. *Very important*, edit the "Measure runs . . ." pane to tell BehaviorSpace to record values of %-similar-wanted generated for each run, which is now crucial information (forget to do this and you'll get useless output). Again specify a maximum of 2,000 iterations for this run – we can rerun with more if necessary.Figure 3.10 plots results of this experiment. These are much finer-grained than those in Figure 3.7, which reports essentially the same experiment but with a grid sweep of %-similar-wanted. Most importantly, we see the model is still generating sharp discontinuities in percentages of evolved percent-similar. These discontinuities are not arising from picking a few particular values of %-similar-wanted in a grid sweep. Evolved

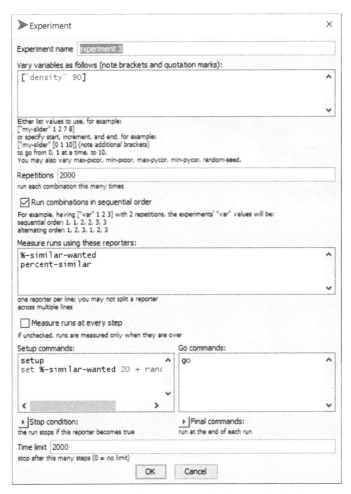

Figure 3.9 BehaviorSpace design screen for Monte Carlo Segregation experiment

social segregation stays the same across wide ranges of values of %-similar-wanted but then suddenly hops up or down. Why?

The answer is simple but important and concerns the model artifact of using eight-cell Moore neighborhoods to decide if agents are happy?. On this assumption, it's only possible to have an integer number of neighbors between zero and eight, just nine possible values. So it's only possible to have a number of similar neighbors with the same nine settings, though you can't have more similar neighbors than you have neighbors. Table 3.3 sets out the full range of possibilities. In the cells it shows the percentage of similar neighbors arising, given a total number of neighbors (in the rows) and a number of similar neighbors (in the columns). This table makes sense of the sharp discontinuities

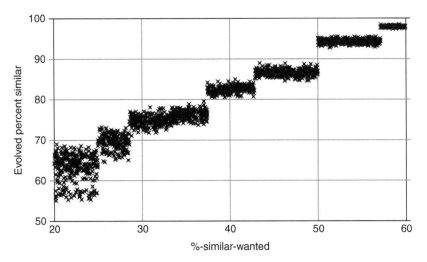

Figure 3.10 Relationship between continuous values of %-similar-wanted and percent-similar achieved, density = 90

in Figure 3.10, identifying thresholds for sudden jumps in evolved social segregation, specified using Moore neighborhoods.

The sudden jump in evolved `percent-similar` when `%-similar-wanted` is 50 makes intuitive sense, but what about when `%-similar-wanted` is about 43, which Figure 3.10 shows is also associated with a sharp discontinuity? Table 3.3 tells you why. When you have seven neighbors (quite common when agent `density` is 90 percent), then if you have three similar neighbors the percentage of neighbors who are similar will be 42.86, or 3/7. Nothing can now change until you have four similar neighbors, so that 4/7 = 57.14 percent of your neighbors are similar. Looking at this the other way, if you have three similar neighbors out of seven and one different neighbor moves away leaving six neighbors in all, the percentage of your neighbors who are similar will jump from 42.86 to 50. You can scour Table 3.3 and see that, given the eight-cell Moore neighborhoods, it is not logically possible to have a proportion of similar neighbors that is greater than 3/7 but less than 1/2. Hence the sharp discontinuity in model outputs that we see at 42.86 `%-similar-wanted`.

Figure 3.11 shows that the discontinuities generated by eight-cell Moore neighborhoods also have a big effect on how hard it is for agents to converge on stable configurations of locations that make them all `happy?`. This figure is directly analogous to Figure 3.8, except we now have continuous values of `%-similar-wanted`, not just a few, and we have lowered `density` a tad from 95 to 90 percent so we have no very long run repetitions that are artificially terminated. We again see

Table 3.3 Percentage of similar neighbors (cells), given total number of neighbors (rows) and number of similar neighbors (columns)

Number of neighbors	0	1	2	3	4	5	6	7	8
0	0								
1	0	100							
2	0	50	100						
3	0	33.33	66.67	100					
4	0	25	50	75	100				
5	0	20	40	60	80	100			
6	0	16.66	33.33	50	66.67	75	100		
7	0	14.29	28.57	42.86	57.14	71.43	85.71	100	
8	0	12.5	25	37.5	50	62.5	75	87.5	100
Number of similar neighbors	0	1	2	3	4	5	6	7	8

the computational wall we begin to hit as we increase the severity of the constraints that must be satisfied to make all agents happy?. However, combined with Table 3.3, Figure 3.11 is much more informative. We see that the wall begins to appear when %-similar-wanted reaches 50, and really kicks with a vengeance when %-similar-wanted hits what we can see from Table 3.3 is 4/7 or 57.14 percent. So, again, the sharp discontinuities in the difficulties facing our agents when they seek spatial locations that make them all happy? are for the most part model artifacts arising from those eight-cell Moore neighborhoods.

Since we don't for one single minute believe that living, breathing people inhabit eight-cell Moore neighborhoods, this is clearly something to be taken care of. The Schelling Segregation model has given us valuable intuitions, but we now see we must satisfy ourselves that these are not artifacts of Schelling's use of Moore neighborhoods to determine whether or not agents are happy?. This is precisely the type of problem we address in the next section, when we modify and extend the NetLogo Segregation model in various ways.

Manipulating More Than One Parameter at Once

Before moving on, however, we circle back and check something we've let slide until now. Does the model parameter, density, make a difference? Perhaps the results we've been getting depend critically on using the default setting of 95 percent for density and might collapse if density takes

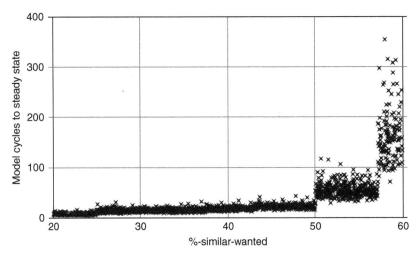

Figure 3.11 Relationship between continuous values of %-similar-wanted and model cycles to stationary state, density = 90

different values. This is substantively important because setting `density` at 95 percent is an entirely arbitrary modeling decision. This has not been calibrated empirically in the sense that our careful observations of the real world have led us to conclude that, on average, five percent of urban housing locations are vacant at any given time. For the moment, this number has just been pulled out of thin air. Worse, whoever coded the model might have chosen it because it gives nicer results than other equally plausible settings. Whenever we see an arbitrary value for a potentially crucial model parameter, we check the robustness of our results to different settings of this. As always, we're going to try and break our results, this time by varying `density` over a wide range.

We also want to take account of the possibility that `density` is more important for some settings of `%-similar-wanted` than for others. It seems on the face of things at least plausible, for example, that `density` will be less important when agents have mild preferences for having similar neighbors than when these preferences are more difficult to satisfy. We therefore need to design an experiment in which we manipulate two things, both `density` and `%-similar-wanted`, at the same time. Figure 3.12 shows a BehaviorSpace design window specifying such an experiment: "experiment 4" in the model **Segregation 1.10**. What's new is the "Vary variables . . . " pane, which we edited to give the following code:

```
["density" [55 10 95]]
["%-similar-wanted" [20 5 55]]
```

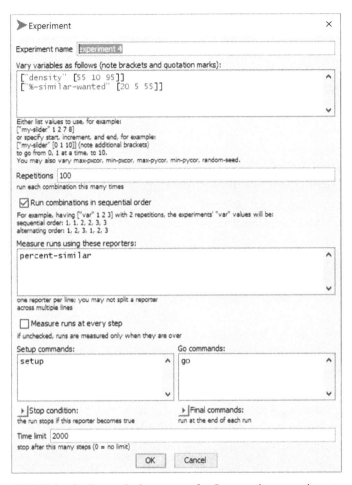

Figure 3.12 BehaviorSpace design screen for Segregation experiment varying two parameters

We're now varying both `density` and `%-similar-wanted` but, instead of typing in all the values of these we want, we've specified a *range* for each variable and an *increment* within this range. The code `["density" [55 10 95]]` asks BehaviorSpace to set `density` in the range 55–95, in increments of 10. Note the extra pair of square brackets. These are needed because, without them, `["density" 55 10 95]` would ask BehaviorSpace to set density at three values: 55, 10, and 95. The extra pair of square brackets tells BehaviorSpace that what is inside is a range of values and an increment within this range. This is easy to forget! In the same way, the code `["%-similar-wanted" [20 5 55]]` sets this variable between 20 and 55 in increments of 5. In total, this specifies five settings of `density` and eight of `%-similar-`

wanted, generating 5 × 8 = 40 different parameterizations of our model. The "Repetitions" pane shows we ask BehaviorSpace for 100 repetitions of each model parametrization, making 4,000 run repetitions in this experiment, a bigger job than before.

So does density make a difference? This is quite difficult to think through logically. We know that lower agent densities, leaving more blank spaces for agents to land on, should make it easier for agents using random moves to find stable configurations of locations that make them all happy? So density should make a difference to *how long* it takes agents to converge on a stable configuration of locations. But will the configurations on which they do converge involve more, or less, social segregation? That's quite a puzzler. We'd prefer to have a firm logical expectation, but we don't, so let's run the experiment and find out.

Figure 3.13 shows some of the results. It's more complicated because what we're doing is more complicated. We could try some fancier mathematical multivariate modeling of these results, using numbers to summarize how evolved percent-similar is affected by both density and %-similar wanted, but Figure 3.13 makes the core intuitions easy to see. It shows four plots of our results, one for each of four different settings of %-similar-wanted. (NB: *ranges* of evolved percent-similar are different for each plot.) The big picture is that varying density makes some, but not a huge difference to results, which on average vary within a two- or three-point range over the very different values of density we investigate.

However, we also see that the *shape* of the relationship between density and evolved percent-similar is different for different values of %-similar-wanted. For some values of %-similar-wanted, for example, 20 and 50, the relationship between density and evolved percent-similar is downward sloping. But for other values, for example, 30 and 40 percent, it is U-shaped. This explains why this interaction was hard to think through logically and shows there is a complex interaction between the combined effects on evolved percent-similar of density and %-similar-wanted. This type of complex interaction is very common when we model the dynamics of social and political behavior.

Finally, we test the conjecture that lower levels of density make it easier for agents to converge on a stable set of locations. Figure 3.14 shows, for two settings of %-similar-wanted, the number of cycles taken to converge on configurations that make all agents happy?.

With %-similar-wanted at the 30 percent default setting of the baseline model, we see in the left panel a distinct if modest increase in time to convergence as density is increased. However, with %-similar-wanted at the

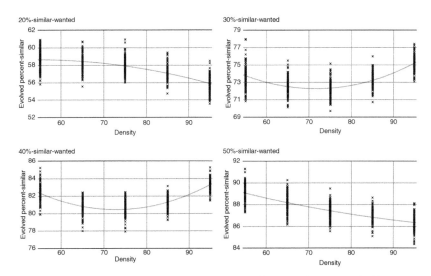

Figure 3.13 Relationship between density and evolved percent-similar, %-similar-wanted 20, 30, 40, 50

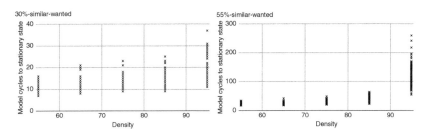

Figure 3.14 Relationship between density and model cycles to convergence, %-similar-wanted 30, 55

highest level we investigated, time to convergence is sharply affected by `density`. The right panel of Figure 3.13 shows the first signs of the computational wall we referred to earlier, but only for the highest level of `density`. So, while it seems generally true that agents converge more quickly on stable locations with lower levels of `density`, this effect is much more striking for higher levels of `%-similar-wanted`.

All of this illustrates the principle that we rarely get the full picture if we confine ourselves to investigating effects of key variables one at a time. *Interactions* between key variables are often a big part of the story. At a practical level we are going to leverage results from Figure 3.13 and 3.14 in the next section. Since decreasing `density` does not make a substantial difference to evolved `percent-similar` (Figure 3.13) but can substantially reduce convergence problems (Figure 3.14), we're going to speed up our computational work by shaving `density` from the baseline 95 percent down to 90 percent. We increase efficiency in this way, knowing that there is no good reason to suppose that one setting of `density` is more realistic than the other.

4 Social Segregation: Extending the Model

We just got serious about modeling social segregation, designing and running computational experiments to exercise the baseline Schelling model in ways that systematically investigate effects of key model parameters. We manipulated the off-the-shelf model but didn't extend or improve it. We now explore ways to improve the model, modify it to incorporate these improvements, then investigate effects of these using new experiments. This is why we do agent-based modeling – to investigate the effects of our own ideas on how best to model important aspects of social interaction. So far we've been finding out how to work agent-based modeling. From now on, things start to get interesting.

We make four types of change to the Schelling model. Each is substantively interesting in itself, but each also teaches us something new about agent-based modeling. First, we allow multiple occupancy of residential spaces. Housing segregation in the real world often leads to substantial variations in, and intensification of, housing densities. For this reason, allowing multiple occupancy of single patches of land seems a very realistic extension of the baseline model. Second, we specify more general social neighborhoods than the eight-cell Moore neighborhoods used in the baseline model, which we have seen generate model artifacts. Again, it seems realistic to assume that the social neighborhoods affecting housing preferences extend beyond a tiny group of immediately proximate neighbors. Third, we relax the unrealistic assumption that all agents are essentially clones of each other, instead assuming that different agents may have different preferences about the numbers of neighbors they prefer to come from the same social group. Finally, we relax the unrealistic assumption that there are only two social groups, generalizing the model to deal with any number of social groups. In the following section we make another important change to the model, allowing for the possibility that even happy people may be forced to move for random reasons that have nothing to do with their local neighborhood.

We make these changes to the baseline model one at a time, going back to the baseline model before we make the next change. We do this because we want to have a clear idea of the effects of each change. If we make two or more changes to the model at the same time, it becomes very difficult to disentangle the effects of each change. In Section 6, however, we investigate an "all-singing, all-dancing" version of the segregation model that makes many changes at the same time in search of increased realism. As we'll see when we get there, while we might think of this as the most realistic version of our model, we'll also find it the hardest to interpret and learn from in a systematic way.

Crowding: Multiple Occupancy of Residential Spaces

The baseline Schelling segregation model does not allow more than one agent to live on a single patch of land. This is by no means a requirement imposed by NetLogo in particular or by agent-based modeling in general. The "one-agent-per-patch" rule was used, without being stated, in Schelling's original segregation model, then faithfully copied into the NetLogo implementation of this. This is a *crucial* substantive assumption about the social world hidden in the model's code in the find-new-spot procedure: if any? other turtles-here [find-new-spot]. This tells unhappy agents who are looking for a new spot to keep on looking if the spot they find is already occupied. We can change this with a single keystroke by commenting out that particular line of code with a ";". Then ;if any? other turtles-here [find-new-spot] becomes a comment and not part of the model. We leave it there so we can clearly see what we have just done. *Adding this single keystroke gives us a completely different model*, allowing agents to move to a new location even when this is already occupied.

This is superficially more realistic, but wrong. We fixed one thing in the model but inadvertently broke something else. This will happen time and time again when you develop an agent-based model and requires continual vigilance. Worse, the new code runs perfectly and gives completely interpretable, but misleading, results. This reminds us that, paradoxically, the best problems are those that crash the model, because we then know for sure we have something to fix and have a reasonable idea what this is. Mistakes like this in the code that leave it running perfectly and don't generate weird results are the most insidious and dangerous in any computational work.

The problem here is a sneaky one. By allowing multiple occupation of patches we've now allowed multiple occupation of patches *by different social groups*. This is not a situation ever encountered by the baseline model, which outlaws multiple occupancy. As a result, allowing multiple occupation of patches means that the baseline model's update-turtles procedure for deciding whether agents are happy? is now simply wrong:

```
set similar-nearby count (turtles-on neighbors) with [color = [color] of
    myself]
```

```
set other-nearby count (turtles-on neighbors) with [color != [color] of
   myself]
set total-nearby similar-nearby + other-nearby
set happy? similar-nearby >= (%-similar-wanted * total-nearby / 100)
```

The problem does not leap out at you, but you see it if you think carefully about the code. The `similar-nearby` and `other-nearby` agent variables are set according to the number of agents on *neighboring* patches. But the NetLogo expression `neighbors` *does not include the calling agent's own patch*. This means that *other* agents on the calling agent's own patch, from the same or a different group, are ignored when setting the agent's happiness. This cannot be right and we need to fix it, even though the unfixed code runs perfectly.

CAUTIONARY TALE! REMOTE BAD EFFECTS OF CODE CHANGES

Small changes in the code at one location intended to modify the model in some way may trigger hard-to-see problems elsewhere with unintended effects.

In this case, improving the code in one procedure to allow multiple occupancy of patches causes problems in another procedure, which has instructions assuming single occupancy.

We fix this using the NetLogo expression `turtles-here`, which lists all agents on the same patch as the calling agent (including the calling agent). Replace the original code with the following:

```
set total-nearby count turtles-on neighbors + count other turtles-here
let similar-here count other turtles-here with [color = [color] of myself}
let similar-there count (turtles-on neighbors) with [color = [color] of myself]
set similar-nearby similar-here + similar-there
set happy? similar-nearby >= (%-similar-wanted * total-nearby / 100)
```

Hopefully, you should by now find this new code reads transparently. Note that `count other turtles-here` excludes the calling agent, which is what we want to do, whereas `count turtles-here` would include the calling agent. We snip `other-nearby` out of the baseline code because, with large numbers of runs, we don't want the machine to be continually calculating something it never uses. We use two `let` instructions, introduced in the previous section, to clarify what would otherwise be a rather complicated `set similar-nearby` instruction. The first `let` calculates the number of similar agents on the calling agent's own patch. The second `let` calculates the number of similar agents on neighboring patches. We can then add these two numbers together to `set similar-nearby`. This now gives us the total number of similar *other* agents on the calling agent's own patch plus those on neighboring patches, which is what we want. We do not need to change set happy?.

There are two more things to do before running the model. We now allow many agents to occupy the same patch, opening up interesting and previously ignored features of social segregation. We can now think of crowding and measure *how many* agents occupy the same patch. The more agents per patch, the more crowded the patch, the greater the local housing density. We suspect that, the more that agents want to live close to others from the same social group, the greater the crowding, or housing density. This new intuition from the Schelling model is easy to investigate.

The number of agents on each patch is: [count turtles-here] of patches. We can summarize these counts over all patches. We compute the maximum level of crowding we observe as: max [count turtles-here] of patches. The average level of crowding is: mean [count turtles-here] of patches. Remembering that the best code is always as modular as possible, breaking out everything into bite-sized pieces, the most elegant way to calculate these numbers in NetLogo is to do something new, which is to define some *reporters*. The nice thing about this, apart from the fact that our new reporters are out there in plain sight and easy to read, is that a reporter holds code that runs and reports results when, but only when, we ask it to. This means that, when we run experiments and only want results at the end of each run, we only have to call the reporters then rather than slow things down by recalculating everything all of the time. We use to-report, finishing with end, to define two new reporters at the end of the code:

```
to-report max-crowding
    report max [count turtles-here] of patches
end
to-report mean-crowding
    report mean [count turtles-here] of patches with
    [count turtles-here > 0]
end
```

Now if we use max-crowding in our code, this will run the to-report max-crowding procedure and report the results. Note that we tweaked the mean-crowding reporter by adding the condition with [count turtles-here > 0]. This is because we want to measure the average level of crowding only of *occupied* patches. We don't want the average diluted by averaging across all patches, including those that are unoccupied. As a final flourish, we add two new monitors to the interface, showing the results of our two new reporters. When we run our model from the interface, we can watch how these measures evolve during a run. When we are doing serious work using BehaviorSpace and want everything running as fast as possible, and we always do, we turn off screen updates and only call these reporters at the end of each run.

Be sure to save the new model under a new name, for example, **"Segregation 2.10 multi occupancy."** Now run the model on the interface. The first time you run any modified model, *always run it with the default settings from the baseline model you just modified,* in this case with density set to 95 and %-similar-wanted set to 30. This gives you the best sense of whether the changes you made have affected key model outputs. Do this and you'll see a screen looking like the one shown in Figure 4.1.

You see your new reporters in the new monitors at the bottom of the screen, showing in this case that agents converged on stable locations that made them all happy? with at most four agents on any one patch and on average 1.21 agents on occupied patches. The %-similar monitor tells a new story,

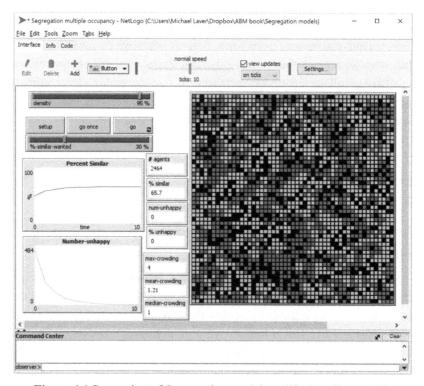

Figure 4.1 Screenshot of Segregation model modified to allow multi-occupancy: default settings

however. It shows that our agents converged on a configuration of stable locations in which, on average, 66 percent of agents on a neighboring, or the same, patch were from the same social group. In the previous section we rigorously estimated the average value of evolved `percent-similar` at about 75 percent, using the baseline model with exactly the same parameter settings but banning multi-occupancy. This is much higher than the 66 percent we find here. Keep clicking setup and run with the multi-occupancy extension of the model as often as you like and you will never generate a value of `percent-similar` that comes close to 75 percent. *Allowing multi-occupancy makes a big difference.* At least for these parameter settings it generates substantially less social segregation. As we will now see, this is not the full story. But one important theoretical finding is now clear. *The hidden assumption that effectively outlaws multiple occupancy is a significant driver of key results from the baseline Schelling model.*

Drag the `%-similar-wanted` slider up to 80 percent, then set up and run the model. You see something like the screen shown in Figure 4.2. Four interesting things have happened. First, now that your model allows multiple occupancy of patches, agents quickly converge on stable locations that make them all `happy?`, even when `%-similar-wanted` is set so high, at 80 percent, that convergence is next to impossible under the baseline model's single-occupancy assumption. It would be a theoretically significant finding if *multiple occupancy makes it easier to make all agents happy*, defining happiness as Schelling does. We will shortly design a computational experiment to investigate this conjecture systematically.

Second, *much* higher levels of housing density, involving a maximum of 26 agents per patch, were necessary in this case to make every agent `happy?`. This is also theoretically important. It tells us that, *while multiple occupancy does allow agents to satisfy even quite extreme preferences for living close to similar neighbors, the price they pay for this is very high levels of housing density.* We also confirm this with a computational experiment, reported below. This finding raises an important new substantive question, which is whether agents might be made unhappy by being forced to experience very high levels of multiple occupancy. Answering this question takes us well beyond the Schelling model, which shielded us from it by banning multiple occupancy. If this interests you, you should think about a more radical modification of the Schelling model, specifying a plausible way in which living in high-density housing reduces agent happiness, while maintaining the condition that living close to similar neighbors increases this.

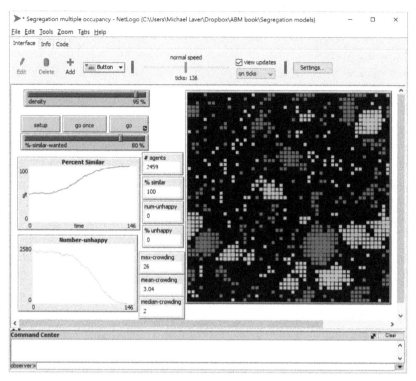

Figure 4.2 Screenshot of Segregation model modified to allow multi-occupancy with `%-similar-wanted` = 80 and many lonely agents

Third, there is now *total* segregation in the evolved configuration of agents' housing locations: evolved `percent-similar` is 100 percent. Theoretically, this tells us that *whether allowing multiple occupancy increases or decreases evolved housing segregation depends crucially on agents' preferences for similar neighbors*, on `%-similar-wanted`. We map out this effect in a computational experiment, reported below.

Fourth, we see many lonely agents in Figure 4.2, red or green agents surrounded by empty black space, showing they have no neighbor at all. How can these people *possibly* be happy if they want 80 percent of their neighbors to be like them but have no neighbors at all? As always, the answer lies in the code. In this case, the code turns out to be hiding an odd assumption we haven't noticed before because, with `density` at 95 percent and multiple occupancy banned, there wasn't enough room in the world for lots of lonely agents, each surrounded by empty space. But now, given all the patches occupied by multiple agents, many more must be left empty, opening up the possibility of solitary agents surrounded by empty space. The code setting these lonely agents to be happy? is unchanged from the baseline model:

```
set happy? similar-nearby >= (%-similar-wanted * total-nearby / 100)
```

Lonely agents have no neighbors and live alone on their patch, so both total-nearby and similar-nearby are zero. The code sets the Boolean variable happy? to "true" whenever $0 >= 0$ is true, which is always the case. The machine faithfully and repeatedly executes the code without error, assuming this is exactly what the coder intended.

Whether or not this is wrong depends entirely on your *substantive* interpretation of the model and raises important theoretical issues. You might interpret Schelling's original model of social segregation, implemented in this code, as a model of how prejudice causes segregation, interpreting prejudice negatively as *not wanting to live with neighbors from different groups*. But you might instead interpret it as a model of homophily or affinity, interpreted positively as *wanting to live with neighbors from similar groups*. These are *not* two sides of the same coin, and lonely agents highlight the difference. If we assume that people dislike living with different neighbors, then it does not seem peculiar to think of them as being happy? if they are lonely and have no neighbors. Living in splendid isolation halfway up a mountain with no neighbor at all is one way to be quite certain you have no neighbor who differs from you. All those lonely but happy people generated by the model make sense on this assumption. If on the other hand we make the more positive assumption of homophily, that agents do not *dislike* living next to people from different social groups but *like* living with at least some neighbors from the same group, then it does seem peculiar to define lonely people as being happy.

Your response to this is a substantive theoretical decision with no right or wrong answer. If you make the negative assumption that people desire not to live with different neighbors, then all those lonely people make sense and you can leave the code just as it is. If you make the positive assumption that people are gregarious but want at least some neighbors to be like themselves, then happy but lonely people make no sense and you need to fix the model. Fortunately, there is a simple hack that does this. There are more correct but cumbersome ways to do it, involving conditional instructions that explicitly set happy? to "false" if the agent has no neighbors. But a hack with the same effect is:

```
set happy? similar-nearby >= (%-similar-wanted *
  (total-nearby + 0.000000001) / 100)
```

This has the effect that we never multiply %-similar-wanted by zero, even when total-nearby is zero. Now, if both similar-nearby and `total-nearby` are zero and the agent is lonely, the inequality will be "false" because of that tiny added 0.000000001, which makes no material difference to any other calculation. (Feel free to add more zeros after the decimal place if you want, though keep the number less than 15, given the precision with which NetLogo does its arithmetic.) This hack is the very opposite of elegant, but it does the trick and runs fast. I leave you the more elegant solution as a programming exercise!

HACKS! DO AS I SAY, NOT AS I DO

In general do not hack your model code as I just did, with an inelegant if effective fix to some problem. This is both aesthetically offensive and unfriendly to third-party readers of your code.

If you really must hack, be sure to add a comment explaining how your hack works, since its effect will typically not read self-evidently to others or even to your own future self.

The Segregation model is grounded intellectually on the notion of "similar wanted", in terms of affinity with others from the same group as opposed to dislike of others from different groups. We'll therefore run an experiment with the positive assumption of homophily, implemented with our hack, saved under the name of "**Segregation 2.11 multi-occupancy no loners**." As you explore ever more agent-based models, you'll find that many of them are driven, under the hood, by a similar assumption of homophily. Set up and run this model once and you'll see something like the screen shown in Figure 4.3. This looks quite different from the screen in Figure 4.2.

All those lonely agents have kept moving until they found some similar neighbors and are no longer scattered throughout the space. The model took longer to converge, 311 instead of 136 iterations, but there are still some occupied patches surrounded by empty space – for example, the red patch near the bottom right corner (at 15 east and –12 south, to be precise). Did we leave some horrible error in the code?

Thankfully, the answer is no. To check this, we learn something new, which will be very useful when you write new models and want to see what's happening to patches and agents. You can take a closer look at any patch or agent in the NetLogo world by moving the cursor directly over the patch and right clicking. You will then see a lot of useful information about that patch. In this case you'll be relieved to find that this isolated patch is in fact *inhabited by more than one similar agent,* two in this case, to be precise. The same is true for the other isolated patches. The model is behaving exactly as we intended, at

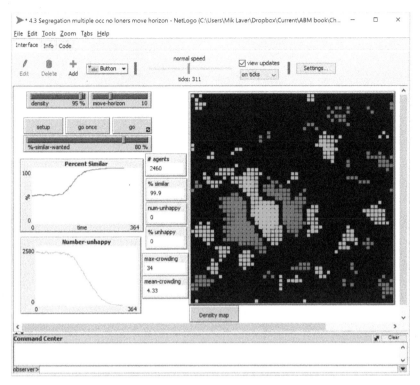

Figure 4.3 Screenshot of Segregation model modified to allow multi-occupancy but no loners with %-similar-wanted = 80

least in this respect, since we do intend our agents to be happy? if they live on an isolated patch not all on their own but with other similar agents.

As a final flourish before getting down to serious simulation runs, we'll program a way to make the map of the NetLogo world not only look nicer but be more informative about housing density. We do this by putting a "Density map" button on the interface, which runs the following code:

```
ask turtles [set size 0.4]
ask patches [set pcolor scale-color black (count
  turtles-here / max-crowding) 1 0]
```

We first make our agents smaller (set size 0.4), slimming them down so they don't cover the entire patch they sit on. The second instruction is complicated, asking patches to scale their color from black to white according to the number of agents living on them (count turtles-here) as a proportion of the maximum number of agents on any patch (max-crowding). The densest patches are then black, the least dense white, with intermediate densities taking

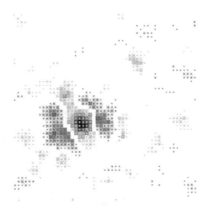

Figure 4.4 Evolved housing density map with density = 95% and %-similar
wanted = 80

shades of gray. (The `scale-color` instruction is fully described in the
NetLogo dictionary.) Hitting the "Density map" button for the evolved pattern
of housing locations in Figure 4.3 gives the map plotted in Figure 4.4, with
darker areas having higher housing densities.

This is exactly the same model, just with prettier output. We put density
scaling under a button rather than embedding it in the code, because we want to
indulge ourselves with a pretty map when the model has converged, but we
don't want to slow down the machine with all that color scaling while the model
is running, especially while we are doing large experiments. The scaling code
runs, once, only when we choose to hit the button. More generally, if you want
to add bells and whistles to your code that are indulgences rather than essentials,
you should handle them this way. Save this model as **Segregation 2.11 multiple
occupancy no loners**.

It's time to give our new model a serious workout. We want to find out how
multiple occupation of housing locations affects evolved patterns of social
segregation. We run precisely the same experiment with the new model that
we ran with the baseline model and reported in Figures 3.10 and 3.11, now also
collecting information from two of our new reporters, `max-crowding` and
`mean-crowding`. We learned from playing casually with the new model that
agents typically converge on stable configurations of housing locations that
make them all happy? even with values of `%-similar-wanted` that are as
high as 80 percent. So we change the relevant BehaviorSpace setup code
for Monte Carlo parameterization of our simulations to `%-similar-
wanted 20 + random-float 60`. This allows us to investigate effects of
parameter settings in the previously unmanageable 60–80 range for `%-
similar-wanted` but does not in any way change agent behavior for the

previously investigated 20–60 range, which is nested in our new experiment. To allow our results to have the same granularity as the previous experiment, we increase the number of run repetitions by 50 percent, to 3,000. This gives us experiment 5 in the **Segregation 2.11 model**. Figure 4.5 directly compares results with identical parameter settings for the baseline model with single occupancy of patches (top panel, repeating Figure 3.10) and the model allowing multiple occupancy (bottom panel).

We see at once that a model allowing multiple occupation generates different evolved levels of social segregation. Compare typical levels of evolved segregation for the default parameter setting of 30 for %-similar-wanted. We saw in the previous section that evolved segregation levels average 75 percent in the baseline model, and the top panel of Figure 4.5 shows they never dip below about 72 percent. When multiple occupancy is allowed, however, evolved levels of segregation with %-similar-wanted set to 30 are distributed around 70 percent. Allowing multiple occupancy in this case results in *less* social segregation. However, if we look at levels of segregation with %-similar-wanted set to 50, we see the opposite pattern; typical levels of segregation are *higher* with multiple occupancy. The segregation curve, the rate at which housing segregation increases as %-similar-wanted increases, is steeper with multiple occupancy, starting with lower levels of segregation but ending with higher levels. This is an interesting substantive finding from the new model.

Figure 4.6 compares models in terms of the speed with which agents converge on a stable configuration of locations making them all happy?, showing big differences between models. The top panel (same as Figure 3.11) reminds us that the baseline model began to hit a computational wall when %-similar-wanted passed the 57 percent threshold identified in Table 3.3. It became computationally intractable once %-similar-wanted passed the 75 percent threshold, effectively never converging despite the fact that, theoretically, there are extraordinarily rare configurations of agent locations to which it would eventually converge.

The bottom panel of Figure 4.6 shows that the model with multiple occupancy breezes through these constraints and converges quite quickly even when the range of %-similar-wanted is extended to 80. The reason for this is simple. Multiple occupancy opens up *many* more possible configurations of agent locations that make them all happy? We do see the beginning of the wall at this point, and I can tell you that the model with multiple occupancy becomes computationally intractable once %-similar-wanted moves into the mid-80s.

An important lesson here is that small and substantively reasonable changes in assumptions can make a big difference to a model's computational tractability, measured in terms of time taken to converge on some stationary state. In

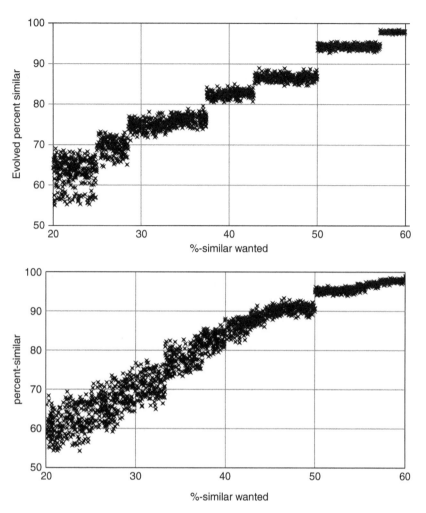

Figure 4.5 Relationship between `%-similar-wanted` and `percent-similar` after convergence, density = 90. Top panel: baseline model. Bottom panel: model with multiple occupancy but no loners

this case the baseline segregation model's assumption of only one agent per patch *is not only substantively unrealistic but also makes the model much more intractable computationally than models based on the more realistic assumption allowing multiple occupancy of the same patch of land.*

Enabling multiple occupancy of patches opens up the possibility of crowding. A substantively important feature of housing segregation is that people from the same social group can become tightly packed together in local areas with very high housing densities, which we might think of as ghettos. We were systematic about measuring housing density in our simulations, recording both max-

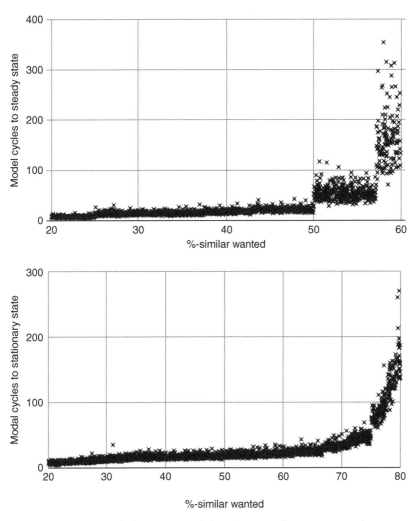

Figure 4.6 Relationship between model cycles to stationary state and percent-similar wanted, density = 90: top panel, baseline model; bottom panel, model with multiple occupancy

`crowding` and `mean-crowding`. Figure 4.7 shows the results. We see two substantively important patterns. First, there is always some crowding once we allow multiple occupancy, even at low levels of `%-similar-wanted`. Second, there is a highly nonlinear relationship between crowding and `%-similar-wanted`. Maximum crowding levels increase only very slightly as we increase `%-similar-wanted` to 60, but then begin to skyrocket. Substantively, this striking new substantive finding derived from the model suggests that, if people have a strong desire to live alongside others from the

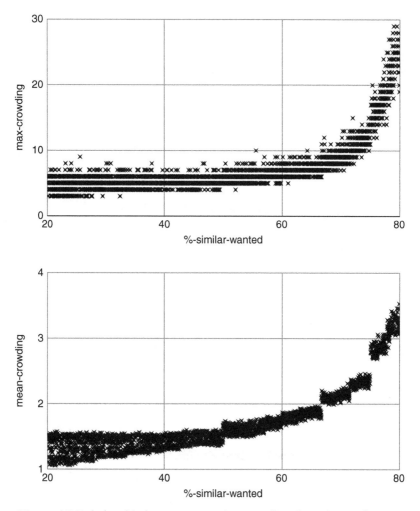

Figure 4.7 Relationship between mean (top panel) and maximum (bottom panel) crowding and %-similar-wanted, density = 90 model with multiple occupancy but no loners

same social group, then there is a threshold after which very high-density housing zones become much more likely. The new model has given us a new intuition about evolved patterns of social segregation.

In a nutshell, allowing multiple occupancy makes a *substantial* difference to the Schelling segregation model, changing most of the headline findings associated with this. Evolved levels of segregation are quite different, and higher levels of %-similar-wanted can be accommodated by stable configurations of housing locations. This is possible because multiple occupancy allows agents to congregate in small regions of high-density housing, since we now have a model that, unlike the baseline Schelling Segregation model, comprehends variations in the density as well as the social segregation of housing.

Larger Social Neighborhoods

The baseline segregation model often predicts sharp discontinuities in evolved levels of social segregation, seen, for example, in Figure 4.5. It seems plausible that these are caused by the Shelling model's assumption that all social interaction is confined to hyperlocal eight-patch Moore neighborhoods. Since real humans do not live in eight-patch Moore neighborhoods, these discontinuities may well be model artifacts, which do not reflect the real world. Real social neighborhoods come in many shapes and sizes, which we will never capture in any general model of social interaction. However, we can take a step toward a more general model by specifying social neighborhoods in terms of some radius from an agent's current location. This radius is a new and substantively important model parameter, specifying social neighborhoods of different sizes. Doing this once again implements a key principle of good modeling. Take an *implicit* model parameter, in this case hard coded in the eight cells of the Moore neighborhood built into NetLogo, and move it into plain sight. Make it an *explicit* parameter, which we can vary systematically to see whether it affects model outputs.

MODELING BEST PRACTICE! NEVER HARD-CODE MODEL PARAMETERS

Never hide potentially important model parameters in the code.

This is what happens if you hard-code them.

Not only does this inadvertently hide potentially crucial model parameters from other users, which is clearly bad practice . . .

. . . it also means you must edit the model code if you want to change parameter settings, which is a *terrible* practice.

All model parameters should be explicit, out there in plain sight and open to manipulation.

So modify the baseline segregation model to specify social neighborhoods of varying sizes. First, add a new global variable, nabe, set with a new slider on the interface. This specifies the radius of the agents' local neighborhoods. We declare a new agent-specific (turtles-own) variable, locals, to hold the identities of other agents currently located less than distance nabe from the calling agent. (NetLogo won't let you use neighbors for your new variable's name because it already has a built-in variable called neighbors.)

Now modify the update-turtles procedure. First, identify each agent's locals with: set locals other turtles in-radius nabe. (I'm unable to stop myself from noting that NetLogo instructions strongly resemble "newspeak" in George Orwell's *1984*. This is not accidental, since newspeak is a radically reduced-form version of English that conveys clear instructions but abolishes all ambiguity and nuance.) The useful NetLogo function `in-radius` reports the identities of all agents within a certain radius, `nabe` in this case, of the calling agent. Having identified the `locals` of each agent, simply replace `neighbors` in the baseline model code with `locals`, giving:

```
set similar-nearby count locals with color = [color] of myself]
set total-nearby count locals
set happy? similar-nearby >= (%-similar-wanted * total-nearby / 100
```

Save this model as **Segregation 2.12 Euclidean neighborhoods**. Before we design and run experiments to investigate effects of neighborhood size on evolved levels of social segregation, we pause to note a very important feature of the new model. While it substantially extends the baseline segregation model, it also nests this. There are parameter settings for the new model that make it behave in *exactly* the same way as the baseline model. If we set `nabe` to 1.5 (in fact, to any number greater than $\sqrt{2}$ and less than 2), then the list of `locals` will be precisely the list of `neighbors` in the eight-patch Moore neighborhood. The horizontally and vertically adjoining patches are distance 1 from the calling agent. The diagonally adjoining patches are, from Pythagoras' theorem, distance $\sqrt{2}$ from the calling patch. The next-closest patches are distance 2 away either vertically or horizontally. Nesting the baseline model in the new model is important because this allows us to check that the new model delivers exactly the same results in exactly the same situation – that we didn't inadvertently change something about the model that we didn't mean to change. As we see from Figure 4.8, setting `nabe` to 1.5 generates an evolved level of segregation well within the range we generated with the baseline model. Having satisfied ourselves that the baseline model is nested inside the new model, we now design our experiment.

MODELING BEST PRACTICE! NEST MODEL EXTENSIONS

When you extend a model by adding a new model parameter, always ensure there is a setting of this parameter that allows you to replicate the original model exactly.

Run the modified model with this setting to ensure that your code changes have not changed the model in some unwanted way.

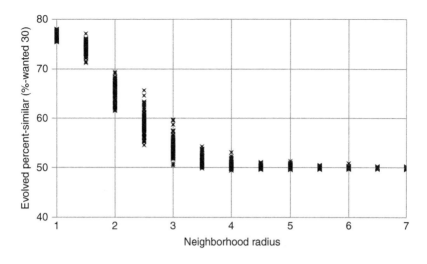

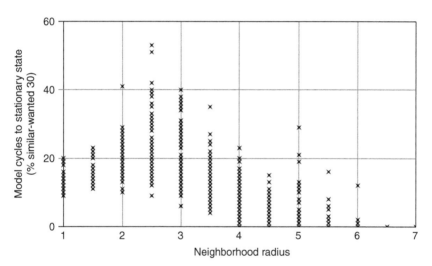

Figure 4.8 Evolved social segregation (top panel) and model cycles to stationary state (bottom panel) for neighborhoods of different sizes: %
`similar-wanted` = 30

We design this experiment as a grid sweep, since, as we just saw, we're *very* interested in model outputs for at least one particular parameter setting – when `nabe` is set to 1.5, nesting the baseline model. (When `nabe` is set to 1 we get the von Neumann neighborhood comprising only the four vertically or horizontally adjoining patches.) Furthermore, while we generalized the notion of a local neighborhood, this is still realized within NetLogo in terms of a rectangular grid of patches. Moving horizontally or vertically at least, effective neighborhood sizes increase in one-unit increments rather than continuously. In the "Vary variables pane" of the BehaviorSpace design window, take account of these increments by sweeping nabe in half-patch increments from 1 to 7, which incorporates 1.5 as a setting to replicate the baseline model. This gives ["nabe" [1 0.5 7]].

This time, however, we vary *two* model parameters rather than just one. We do this because we have theoretical reasons to expect the relationship between neighborhood size and evolved levels of social segregation to depend on %-similar-wanted. For example, since on average 50 percent of agents come from each social group, we know that, when social neighborhoods become sufficiently large and certainly when the social neighborhood is the entire NetLogo world, it is not logically possible to satisfy all agents if they all want more than 50 percent of their neighbors to come from the same group. When neighborhood size is so large that it includes the entire NetLogo world, the evolved level of social segregation in each agent's neighborhood must be the 50 percent-similar we know to exist in that world. Obviously in this situation, therefore, agents who want 60 percent-similar can never all be happy?. This is another good example of why we should always think logically about what to expect from our model rather than simply firing it up to see what happens.

For every setting of nabe, therefore, we specify four different settings of %-similar-wanted (30, 40, 50, 60) in the BehaviorSpace "Vary variables" pane. Setting %-similar-wanted to 30 replicates our baseline model runs. Setting it to 60 specifies a model parameterization that we know can never satisfy all agents when neighborhood size becomes sufficiently large. Given the grid of rectangular patches arranged on a torus, however, it is difficult (for me at least) to determine logically how large *sufficiently* large might be.

We now have an experiment that specifies 13 different settings of nabe, 4 settings of %-similar-wanted, and 100 repetitions of each run. This gives $13 \times 4 \times 100 = 5,200$ run repetitions in all. This is experiment 6 in the model **Segregation 2.12**. This is many more than the 1,000 repetitions we have been using to date, so the experiment will take much longer to run on your computer, especially since the model will run a lot slower as neighborhood size increases. But you can run it overnight while you sleep peacefully. Then it will take no time at all out of your waking life.

Results of the experiment for the out-of-the-box setting of %-similar-wanted at 30 are summarized in Figure 4.8. The top panel shows evolved levels of social segregation for social neighborhoods of different sizes. First, note that the expanded model has indeed systematically nested the baseline model. When nabe is 1.5, we see the same levels of evolved percent-similar, at around 75 percent, as for the baseline. Second, note the distinctly nonlinear relationship, with segregation declining steeply as neighborhood size increases, then gradually (asymptotically) approaching what we have just seen is the logical lower bound of 50 percent-similar when neighborhoods are so large they include the entire NetLogo world. By the time neighborhood radius has increased to 5, evolved levels of segregation are indeed indistinguishable, at around the 50 percent level of the original random scatter, from those we observe for much larger social neighborhoods. This is because it is very easy to satisfy all agents as neighborhood size increases if they want only 30 percent of their neighbors to be like themselves.

The bottom panel of Figure 4.8 throws further light on this. It shows, for different neighborhood sizes, how long it took agents to converge on a configuration of locations making them all happy?. Again we see a nonlinear relationship, but the striking finding here is that, once neighborhood size hits 6.5, it takes *zero* model cycles to make all of our agents happy?. They are always happy? with the original random scatter. We therefore see that, if %-similar-wanted is 30, the sufficiently large size for social neighborhoods is 6.5.

These are striking findings. They show that the "talking point" intuition from the Schelling segregation model, which is that surprisingly high levels of social segregation can evolve even when agents prefer only a much smaller proportion of similar neighbors, is to a large extent a function of the model's hyperlocal eight-cell Moore neighborhoods. Expanding the size of these neighborhoods but holding %-similar-wanted constant at 30, we quickly arrive at evolved levels of social segregation that are as low as we can logically achieve, given that 50 percent of agents are in each social group.

This is interesting, but the nonlinear relationships shown in Figure 4.8 are untypically smooth and pretty. Figure 4.9 is analogous to Figure 4.8 except that %-similar-wanted has been raised to 40. It includes results from an additional experiment taking neighborhood size up to 15, since it was clear that evolved levels of social segregation had not begun to approach what we have seen is their theoretical limit of 50 by the time neighborhood size had reached 7. The top panel of Figure 4.9 shows a sharp discontinuity. As neighborhood size increases, evolved levels of social segregation first rise, peaking when neighborhood size is between 5 and 7. They begin to decline as neighborhood size increases beyond this, but something else also begins to happen. With the larger neighborhood sizes, some initial random scatters of agents, or very small movements from these, now satisfy all agents who want 40 percent of the neighbors to come from the same group. As neighborhood size increases beyond 8, since on average 50 percent of agents belong to each social group,

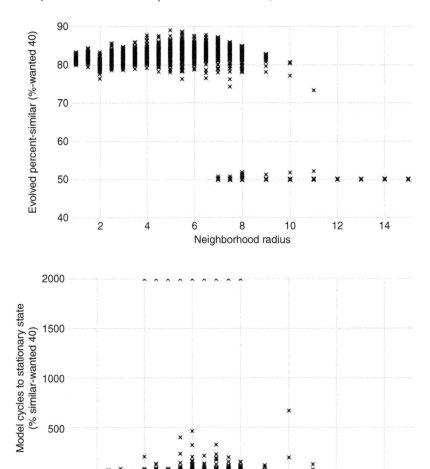

Figure 4.9 Evolved social segregation (top panel) and model cycles to stationary state (bottom panel) for neighborhoods of different sizes: `%-similar-wanted = 40`

it becomes progressively much easier to satisfy all agents with 40 `%-similar-wanted`. In fact, by the time neighborhood size has reached 12, all initial random scatters of agents satisfy this condition, with all run repetitions generating evolved levels of social segregation at about the 50 percent logical lower bound. Strikingly, no setting of neighborhood size generates middling levels of social segregation in this model.

This is another interesting finding, further highlighted by the bottom panel of Figure 4.9. For neighborhood sizes between 4 and 8, it becomes *much* harder to

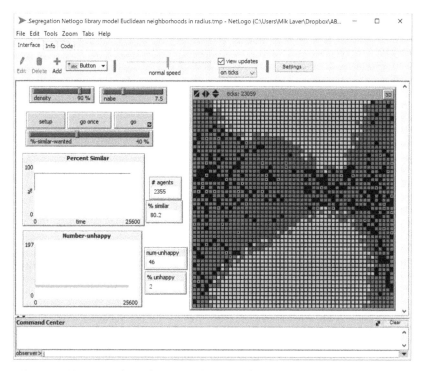

Figure 4.10 Screenshot of Segregation model with neighborhood size of 7.5 and %-similar-wanted = 40

satisfy all agents if they have 40 %-similar-wanted. Many run repetitions were terminated at 2,000 cycles, leaving some agents still not happy?. By the time neighborhood size had reached 12, however, all model runs were stopping themselves at zero cycles, since all agents were happy? with the initial random scatter.

Figure 4.10 shows a typical screenshot of evolved percent-similar after a run of more than 23,000 model cycles, with nabe set to 7.5 and %-similar-wanted to 40. The plots show that key outputs have flatlined for a long time despite the fact that there are still 46 unhappy green agents always moving restlessly but never finding a location that makes them happy?. The map of the NetLogo world tells us how this happened, showing a configuration of agent locations that can emerge to make it extraordinarily difficult (we're not logically justified in saying *impossible*) for all agents to be happy?.

Most green agents have clustered into a single solid block (wrapping from bottom to top of the world). Since we have reverted to the baseline model assumption that no multiple occupancy is allowed, there is no open space in the green zone into which unhappy green agents can move. These remain unhappily

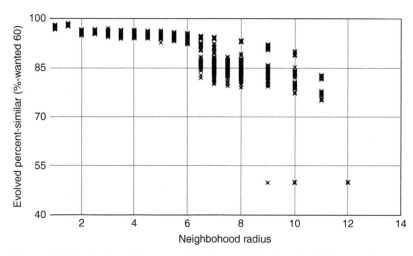

Figure 4.11 Evolved social segregation for neighborhoods of different sizes: `%-similar-wanted`= 60

stuck in gaps inside the red block with nowhere to go that makes them `happy?`. Once neighborhood size becomes large enough, these unhappy green agents will become `happy?` because parts of the large block of `happy?` green agents will now be in their local neighborhood.

We already saw that, since 50 percent of agents belong to each group, if they all want 60 percent of their neighbors to come from the same group, then it is logically impossible for them all to be `happy?` when the social neighborhood is at its maximum possible size – the entire world. We know logically that agent locations will in this event churn forever. While levels of evolved social segregation in Figure 4.11, which plots results when `%-similar-wanted` is set to 60, look quite similar to those in Figure 4.9, there is a huge difference in how the segregation model generates these.

If all agents want `percent-similar` to be 40, then they become increasingly *easy* to satisfy as neighborhood size increases. If they want `percent-similar` to be 60, however, they become increasingly *difficult* to satisfy as neighborhood size increases, at some point becoming logically impossible to satisfy. Evolved levels of social segregation are at their logical minimum of 50 percent when social neighborhood sizes reach 12 in both cases. When `%-similar-wanted` is 40, however, the model is immediately stopping itself because all agents are `happy?` with the random scatter. But when `%-similar-wanted` is 60, the model *never* stops itself, and must be artificially stopped, because agents cannot possibly all be `happy?`. Perhaps paradoxically, evolved levels of social segregation are also at their logical minimum in the latter case, but now only because of the continuous churn of unhappy agents.

Overall, the declines in evolved social segregation implied by our model as neighborhood sizes increase are always nonlinear and rarely smooth. They hit sharp discontinuities, which arise from logical constraints generated by the proportions of agents belonging to each social group. Given these proportions (50 percent in each of two groups in this case, but there are obviously many different assumptions about this), agents may become either very easy or very hard to satisfy as the size of their social neighborhoods increases.

This particular extension of the model only scratches the surface of how we might model social neighborhoods once we move beyond the simple, tractable, but unrealistic device of using eight-cell Moore neighborhoods. The extension suggested here, furthermore, retains an unattractive feature of the baseline model. It assumes there is a bright line around each social neighborhood. On one side of this line, you treat everyone equally as your neighbor and you ignore everyone on the other side of the line. The plausibility of this is an empirical question about how real people feel about their neighbors in the real world. Do next-door neighbors, or those in the same multi-occupied building, impinge on you more than those who live several streets away? A more general account of neighborhood effects might model some kind of decay in the strength of these effects as neighbors become more remote. This will require assumptions about the shape of this decay. Does the strength of the neighborhood effect decline in a linear fashion as distance increases? Or is the decay nonlinear, for example, exponential? Indeed, exponential decay in the strength of the neighborhood effect is an attractive option here. It would model the impact of neighbors as being most intense when they are very close, declining smoothly as neighbors become more distant and getting very close indeed to zero, but never *exactly* zero, with large distances. There would now be no bright line in the neighbor effect, just a smooth decline approaching zero as neighbors become more distant. You can easily use NetLogo's `exp` function to specify exponential decay in the impact of neighbors if they become further way, though you will need to think carefully about the precise nature of this decline.

The bottom-line implication of this extension of the Schelling model is that evolved patterns of social segregation very much depend upon the size of the local neighbourhood, which determines whether or not agents are `happy?`. The larger this neighborhood, the lower the resulting level of evolved social segregation. *The core intuitions usually attributed to the Schelling Segregation model depend critically on the assumption that agents consider only hyperlocal social neighborhoods.*

Move Horizons

Another neighborhood effect in the baseline Schelling model concerns *how far* unhappy people are prepared to move in search of ultimate happiness. This potentially important model parameter is hidden in the baseline model's code as fd random-float 10 in the model's find-new-spot procedure. This confines unhappy agents to seeking a new location within a circle of radius 10 from their current location. But why not 5 or 15? And does this make a difference? This is yet another example of a crucial modeling principle of not *hard-coding model parameters.*

If we have a good theoretical reason to limit agents' moves to some local radius or horizon, and this might be perfectly reasonable, then we should be open and explicit about this. We can easily fix the Segregation model to create a new "horizon" parameter, making this both explicit and manipulable. Declare a new global variable, move-horizon, using a slider on the interface, then change the relevant find-new-spot code to fd random-float move-horizon. Now, instead of hard-coding the maximum agent move radius as 10 and hiding this key parameter in the code, we've made it visible and manipulable, as it always should have been. This parameter definitely makes a difference, as you can see from Figure 4.12, which shows results for a modified version (**Segregation 2.13**) of the model, which allows multiple occupation of patches but no lonely agents (**Segregation 2.11**).

The left panel shows an evolved pattern of housing segregation assuming only tiny local moves by unhappy agents, setting move-horizon to 1; the right panel shows an equivalent pattern of allowing large moves, with move-horizon set to 30. In each case, there is almost total evolved social

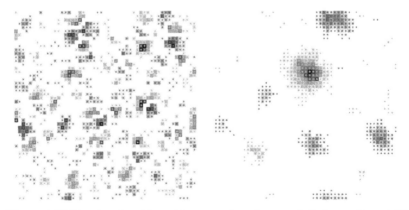

Figure 4.12 Housing densities with move-horizon = 1 (left panel) and 30 (right panel) (density = 95, %-similar-wanted = 80)

segregation, with `percent-similar` almost 100 percent, but the geographic patterns of segregation and evolved housing densities are very different. With small local moves, small local clusters of single-group housing are spread all over the map. With large moves by unhappy agents, the evolved pattern involves a small number of well-separated and larger high-density clusters. Strikingly, while one number, evolved `percent-similar`, tells us there is no difference in model output between the two scenarios, our own two eyes and evolved housing densities tell a different story. Rigorously characterizing the two different geographic patterns of segregated housing in Figure 4.12 is not easy – a common problem with spatial patterns such as this – but we can systematically investigate the relationship between `move-horizon`, `mean-crowding`, and `max-crowding`. Figure 4.13 reports the results of an experiment designed to explore in a systematic way the patterns of evolved housing segregation shown in Figure 4.12.

The same model parameterization was used as for the screenshots in Figure 4.12, except that `move-horizon` was systematically increased, in steps of 1, from 1 to 30 by setting `["move-horizon" [1 1 30]]` in BehaviorSpace. The design for this sketch run, designed to get a feel for things, specified 25 run repetitions, of maximum length 2,000 iterations, per parameter setting, giving 750 run repetitions in all. This is experiment 7 in the model **Segregation 2.13**. Figure 4.13 shows very clearly that evolved housing density depends unambiguously on the `move-horizon` of unhappy agents, rising steadily until `move-horizon` reaches about 15 and then leveling off. Bearing in mind that these findings are for agents who want 80 percent of their neighbors to be from the same social group, mean housing densities are around 2.5 agents per patch, and maximum densities somewhat under 20 per patch when the agents are confined to hyperlocal moves. Both of these numbers essentially double when agents' move-horizons are extended, leading to maximum densities that are often over 40 agents/patch.

We therefore see not only that housing density is a theoretically very interesting outcome of Schellingesque models of housing segregation but that density is affected by more than the intuitively plausible `%-similar-wanted`. Agents' move horizons, hidden and hard-coded in the baseline model, also have a substantial effect on evolved housing densities. This is not an expected or intuitive effect. At least I did not expect, when I first coded this, that increasing agents' move horizons would increase evolved housing densities. This is another reason to be particularly ruthless in exposing hidden and hard-coded model parameters and investigating the effects of these. These effects may be both substantial and unexpected.

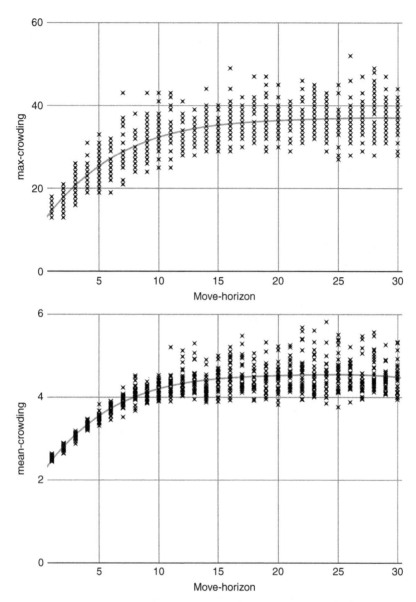

Figure 4.13 Maximum (top panel) and mean (bottom panel) housing density by `move-horizon` (`density = 95`, `%-similar-wanted = 80`). Trend line is a fourth-order polynomial fit

Agents with Varying Preferences

A strikingly unrealistic theoretical assumption of the baseline Schelling Segregation model, and indeed of many published models of social interaction, is that all agents are clones of each other. Specifically in this case, the model treats %-similar-wanted as a *global* variable, identical for all agents. This information about preferences, however, is of its essence a feature of individual agents, one that might very plausibly vary between agents. Real human societies are fundamentally about the coexistence of people with different preferences. Here we might reasonably expect considerable diversity in the extent to which people prefer to live alongside others from the same social group. This, indeed, is a theoretically important feature of human societies that should be part of our model. Diversity of preferences is a key feature of many ABMs and is very easy to build into these.

Modify the baseline segregation model to achieve this by making %-similar-wanted an *agent-specific* rather than a *global* variable. Select and delete the %-similar-wanted slider from the interface. Ignore the pesky error message that pops up because the model's code now refers to something that does not currently exist. Fix this by declaring %-similar-wanted as an agent-specific variable, adding this to the turtles-own list. Now %-similar-wanted can vary between agents, but to make this happen you must now specify *precisely how* you want it to vary. Theoretically, you could make different plausible assumptions about this, but one natural possibility is that the values of %-similar-wanted have a normal distribution across all agents, with a particular mean and standard deviation. I say this assumption is natural because many naturally occurring phenomena have normal distributions or something quite close to these. Another big advantage of this assumption is that it allows us, once again, to nest the baseline model in our new model. By setting the standard deviation of %-similar-wanted to zero, we give all agents the same value of this, in effect treating it as if it were a global variable.

So put two new sliders on the interface, declaring two new global variables: mean-sim-wanted and sd-sim-wanted. Specify a range for the former of 20–80 and for the latter of 0–20. (You might as an exercise ponder why I set those ranges and make your own decisions on this.) Now give every agent a different preference for %-similar-wanted, each drawn randomly from the normal distribution you just specified. Do this for each agent immediately after creating it in the setup procedure:

```
sprout 1 [
  set color one-of [red green]
  set %-similar-wanted random-normal mean-sim-wanted sd-sim-wanted
  if %-similar-wanted > 100 [set %-similar-wanted mean-sim-wanted]
  if %-similar-wanted < 0 [set %-similar-wanted mean-sim-wanted]
    ]
```

The last two lines of code here are *error traps*, a programming device we're meeting for the first time, which can save both you and other users of your code a mountain of grief. These are important here because users can easily set values of mean-sim-wanted and sd-sim-wanted that generate random draws outside the range 0–100. A mean of 30 and a standard deviation of 20 are consistent with many negative values of %-similar-wanted, for example, which make no theoretical sense and generate misleading results when they don't crash the code. These error traps catch all values outside the range 0–100 and replace them with the mean value of this variable. (Strictly speaking, therefore, the distribution %-similar-wanted we specify in the code is no longer normal but rather truncated below 0 and over 100 and biased toward the mean.) We don't need to change anything else in the code to make this fundamental theoretical improvement to the model. Save this model as **Segregation 2.14 similar wanted agent specific**.

First, test the nesting of the baseline model. Set mean-sim-wanted to 30 and sd-sim-wanted to 0. Run the model a few times and check that it gives you the same results as the baseline model. It does. Now we can specify and run an experiment designed to investigate whether the extended model generates systematically different results if %-similar-wanted varies between agents. First, we run an experiment as close as possible to the baseline experiment in Table 3.1, using the NetLogo model's default settings. We do this in the BehaviorSpace design window by specifying ["mean-sim-wanted" 30] and ["density" 95] in the "Vary Variables" pane and using a Monte Carlo parametrization of sd-sim-wanted by putting set sd-sim-wanted random-float 20 at the end of the "Setup commands" pane. This randomly samples sd-sim-wanted in the range 0–20 while keeping the mean of %-similar-wanted the same as in the baseline experiment. This is experiment 8 in the model **Segregation 2.14**, which allows us to investigate what happens when we increase the level of variation in agents' preferences around the baseline mean.

Results of a 1,000-run experiment with this design are shown in Figure 4.14. Two things stand out. First, there is no systematic change, up or down, in evolved levels of social segregation as we increase the variation in our agents' desire to live with similar neighbors. The same levels of social segregation emerge, whether this variation is low or high. We see this clearly if we ask Google Sheets to add a linear trend line to the plot. This is absolutely flat. Second, this trend line helps us see that the average evolved level of segregation is a tad over 72 percent – 72.5 percent for this experiment, to be precise. This contrasts with an average segregation of about 75 percent for the baseline model with otherwise identical parameter settings. This is a small but

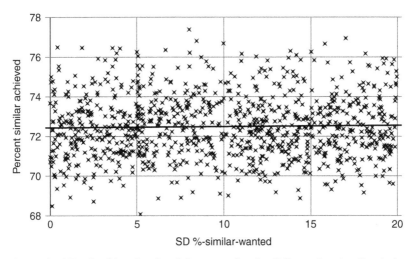

Figure 4.14 Evolved levels of social segregation for different levels of variation in agent preferences (mean 30 %-similar-wanted)

theoretically important substantive difference. *It does make a difference to model social interaction in this setting as taking place between agents with diverse preferences.*

It is not the case, however, that clones are always harder to satisfy than a diverse set of agents. Figure 4.15 reports an experiment analogous to that in Figure 4.14 but with `mean-sim-wanted` set to 50. This is experiment 9 in the model **Segregation 2.14**. With a mean of 50 and a standard deviation varying up to 20, we often randomly draw values of `%-similar-wanted` well above the threshold of 75 percent that we saw earlier makes it very difficult indeed for agents to converge on locations that make them all `happy?`. Results reported in Figure 4.15 come from an experiment with parameter settings tweaked a little to allow it to complete in minutes rather than days or weeks, but unlikely to affect the conclusion. (The range of `sd-sim-wanted` was trimmed to 0–10, and `density` was reduced to 90.) We again see no systematic relationship between the level of variation in agents' preferences and evolved levels of social segregation, another flat linear trend line. However, echoing our findings in Figure 4.6, the average level of evolved social segregation with varying agent preferences is now *higher* (at a tad over 90 percent) than in the baseline model with clones (at about 87 percent) when agents on average want 50 percent or more of their neighbors to come from the same group.

We draw three general conclusions from all of this. First, it is both theoretically desirable and in practice easy to model populations of *agents who are not all clones* but who have preferences varying in systematic ways captured by

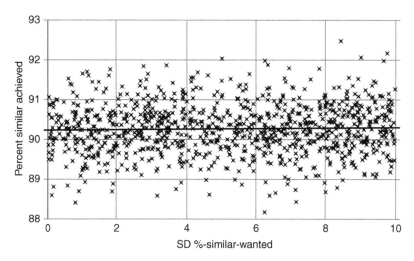

Figure 4.15 Evolved levels of social segregation for different levels of variation in agent preferences (mean 50 %-similar-wanted)

model parameters. There is, however, a cost to doing this. Specifying variation in agents' preferences increases the number of parameters. In this case one global parameter, `%-similar-wanted`, becomes two: `mean-sim-wanted` and `sd-sim-wanted`. This gives us parameterized variation in agents' preferences, which is good, but the extra parameter makes our model more complicated, which has a cost. Theoretically speaking, model output will harder to understand; practically speaking, we substantially increase the amount of computational work needed to map out model results. Here, for every level of `mean-sim-wanted`, we must now map out effects of different levels of `sd-sim-wanted`. This cost is worth paying within reason. ABMs in which agents are all clones of each other are not simply less realistic than those describing populations with diverse preferences; they may generate atypical results.

The second important lesson here is that *negative results are good, too.* Whatever our theoretical intuitions about how increasing the diversity of agents' preferences might affect evolved levels of social segregation, Figures 4.14 and 4.15 send a clear message. While having *some* diversity does make a difference to model results, an important finding, *more* diversity does not generate more, or less, evolved segregation. We might speculate theoretically that this is because, as we increase diversity of agent preferences, for every agent who becomes harder to satisfy as a result of having a higher value of `%-similar-wanted`, there is typically another who becomes easier to satisfy as a result of having a lower value of this. Such a negative finding is just as important as it would have been had we found that increasing agents' preference diversity makes a big difference. This was clearly something worth checking, and now we know the answer. When you generate null results using ABMs, or indeed any other technology, report them, don't hide them! They add to the stock of knowledge.

Finally, we see that changing the model does indeed change key results, not always in the same direction. Whenever you change a model in a way you think is important and worth reporting, you typically need to do quite a bit of computational work before you can systematically map out all the effects of this change. We only scratched the surface here with the experiments reported in Figures 4.14 and 4.15. As an exercise, you might care to think of many other experiments that might be informative once we allow preferences to vary systematically between agents.

More Than Two Social Groups

When we played with the model a couple of sections ago, we hacked it to create more than two social groups. The time has come to make this theoretically important improvement to the model in a well-controlled and systematic way. We can then investigate whether the well-known core intuitions from the baseline Schelling Segregation model depend critically on the limitation that it comprehends only two social groups. Are evolved patterns of social segregation the same if there are more, even many more, social groups? It's very easy to modify the baseline model to comprise any number of social groups.

You want to vary the number of social groups in a systematic way, so add this as a new parameter, `n-groups`, to the baseline model. Declare this as a global variable by adding the slider `n-groups` to the interface, specifying a range for this between 2 and 50. As always, the range we specify on the interface for any global variable affects only what we do on the interface. You can set `n-groups` to anything you want in an experiment. To see this in action once you have finished the modifications set out below, type `set n-groups 5000` into the observer window and then hit "setup." The code will faithfully obey you and create twice as many different social groups as there are agents. This makes limited theoretical sense, but the faithful code doesn't care in the slightest about that. Hit "run" and the model runs just fine, though good luck waiting for your agents to converge on a stable configuration of locations that makes them all `happy?` if you leave `%-similar-wanted` at 30! Setting `n-groups` to 2 nests the baseline model inside the extended model.

Now go to the code and, first, add a new agent-specific variable `group` by listing this under `turtles-own`. This stores the number of the group to which each agent belongs. Instead of specifying each agent's group by a `color`, which doesn't scale to large numbers of groups, we now assign each agent a group number. We do this immediately when we create each agent:

```
sprout 1 [
          set group 1 + random n-groups
          set color (15 + 30 * group)]
```

The first instruction gives the agent a random group number between 1 and n-groups. The second instruction is purely cosmetic, to make the interface look nice, and gives each group a different color. We don't want to be picking from a tiresome list of up to 50 different colors, so exploit the fact that NetLogo refers to colors by numbers. You can see these numbers if you go to the "Tools" menu in NetLogo and pick "Color Swatches." These numbers go up to 140 and if you set a color higher than 140, NetLogo deducts 140 from this number. If you just use the group number as a color, you won't be able to see the difference between colors and using colors at all will be pointless. The code set color (15 + 30 * group) is a trick I played around with to get NetLogo to assign colors to groups, using group numbers to pick colors and cycling though quite a wide range of these. *This has no effect whatsoever on how the model runs* but gives different groups different colors on the interface.

You've one more thing to do if you don't want the code to crash in flames. Modify the update-turtles code to replace color with group: [group = [group] of myself] and [group != [group] of myself]. You now have an extended version of the Schelling Segregation model allowing *any number of different social groups*. As always, save your new model as **Segregation 2.15 n-groups**. Set the number of social groups to 50, then hit "setup" and run the model from the interface. The model will churn for a while but finally stop at something like the screenshot in Figure 4.16.

Surprisingly – well, it surprised me, though maybe it doesn't surprise you at all – we see that even with 50 different social groups, agents eventually find a stable configuration of locations that makes them all happy?. The tick counter shows us that this time it took 4105 iterations. The plots show us that the model had nearly converged on a stationary state about halfway through this run, with the remaining 2,000 cycles taken up by a tiny number of unhappy agents who did eventually find a place to live that made them happy?. Looking at the model in motion, you might have thought it was never going to converge. But then, at last, it did! This is a crucial lesson in itself. Patience is a virtue when exploring new agent-based models. It is always dangerous to conclude, impatiently, that the model will never converge. After all, time to convergence of any model is simply a function of available computer power. When I started working in this field years ago, every experiment reported here would have taken

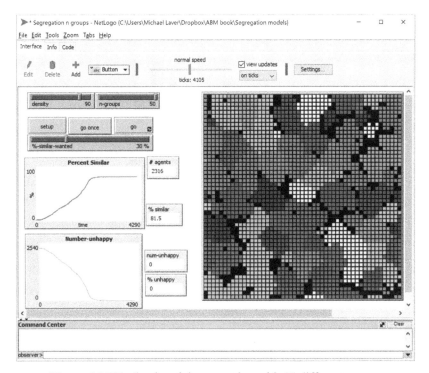

Figure 4.16 Evolved social segregation with 50 different groups

ages longer. In twenty years' time, everything reported here will run in the bat of an eyelid and you'll be able to specify *vastly* more taxing experiments.

You also see that, once all agents are happy?, percent-similar with 50 groups has evolved to over 81 percent, substantially higher than for two groups with the same parameter settings. Be honest, is that what you expected? The first experiment we design for our new model replicates the baseline model in every respect, but investigates effects of the number of social groups. Since the number of groups is an integer, we investigate its effects using a grid sweep. Specify this in Behavior Space with ["n-groups" [2 1 20]]. This asks NetLogo to run through values of n-groups that start with 2 and increase in increments of 1 up to 20. As before, lower density a tad to 90 to make convergence happen more quickly without, as we saw, materially affecting results. Specify 100 run repetitions for each of the 19 different settings of n-groups, giving 1,900 repetitions. This is experiment 10 in the model **Segregation 2.15**.

Once we raise n-groups over 20, things often take a *very* long time to converge, yet results are not hugely different. In the limit, of course, if n-groups is huge and every agent is in a different group, then it's logically

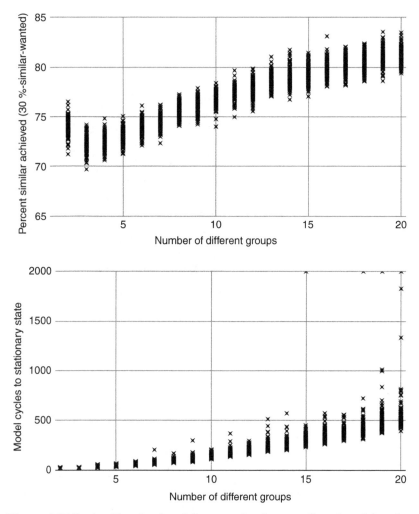

Figure 4.17 Evolved levels of social segregation (top panel) and model cycles to stationary state (bottom panel) with between 2 and 20 different social groups; `%-similar-wanted = 30`

impossible for anyone to be happy?, so things can never converge. We know this theoretically and don't need a centuries-long computer run to confirm it. This is another example of designing computational experiments to investigate effects of parameter values that you expect, for well-thought-out theoretical reasons, to be *interesting*.

Figure 4.17 shows key results. The top panel shows a striking pattern, with social segregation actually *declining* when we move from two groups to three, then increasing steadily as the number of groups rises beyond three.

The two-group Schelling segregation model generates results that are an exception to the general pattern. This is a theoretically and substantively important finding in itself if we want the Schelling model to inform us about social segregation. Most discussions of this model are based on what we now see is an atypical two-group implementation, yet we find more than two social groups in most real-world settings. The main conclusions we draw from the extended model, however, are *stronger* in this case. *As we increase the number of groups beyond three, patterns of evolved social segregation become even sharper.*

Before setting too much store by this conclusion, however, we should take account of other findings in this section. For example, the eight-cell Moore neighborhoods may obviously have a different effect once the number of social groups exceeds eight, though this is hard to think through rigorously. This may be the time to abandon our careful strategy of making only one model extension at a time. It seems on the face of things plausible that the effect of having large numbers of social groups might change if we allow multiple occupancy of patches or larger social neighborhoods. This is why we move in the final section to an "all-singing, all-dancing" version of the segregation model, which lets us simultaneously vary several things at the same time. Not surprisingly, we will see that, while the model is in some sense more realistic if we do this, its output is much harder to understand. This trade-off between realism and intuition runs through any attempt to model social and political interaction, whether using agent-based modeling or any other technology. Before doing any of that, however, we have another important step to take in improving our model, which is to take account of the fact that agents may also behave in random ways that have nothing to do with our model. We do this in the next section.

5 Social Segregation: Stochastic Modeling

A striking feature of every model of social segregation we've built up until now is that they can generate stable configurations of agents in which every agent is happy? For some parameter settings, these configurations may be very rare – as in Figure 2.5 – so agents making random moves typically take an extraordinarily long time to find them. Eventually, however, on an evolutionary timescale they will find them. (By evolutionary timescale I mean a timescale that is extraordinarily, even unimaginably, long – long enough for critical events to happen that are *extremely* unlikely but not logically impossible.) After such a stable configuration emerges, no agent ever wants to move. The social process we model reaches a *stationary* state. Nothing changes or can possibly change, even if we run the model forever. We also saw that different runs of exactly the same model with exactly the same parameter settings typically generate slightly different stationary states, each with slightly different levels of social segregation. If we think about this for a moment, the reason is obvious. Given any particular random scatter of agents at the start of the run, many agents are happy with their locations from the get-go and never want to move. So different starting configurations generate different outcomes. When this happens, we call the process we model *path-dependent*. The fact that the baseline Schelling Segregation model is path-dependent is why we need many different runs of the same model with the same parameter settings, so we can characterize a typical outcome by aggregating results to average out path-dependent variations in particular outcomes.

Social interactions in the real world do not lead to stable outcomes that never, ever, change. The real world is full of change and uncertainty – it is stochastic. For any given state of the world, random stuff happens that has nothing at all to do with the processes we model. This potentially destabilizes the current state of the world and changes the course of social interaction. In relation to social segregation, for example, even perfectly happy people die. Others move house for reasons that have nothing to do with their neighbors, perhaps to take a new job or care for a sick relative. These random events add stochastic components to any model and change it fundamentally. If even the happiest agents move with some probability for exogenous reasons – reasons outside the model – agent locations never reach a stable configuration in which nobody moves. This has the crucial implication that the evolution of agent locations depends much less on their original random scatter. Adding the stochastic component of random moves by happy? agents makes the model much less path-dependent, which in modeling terms is a good thing. Considering both substantive realism and theoretical elegance, it is good to model the possibility of random events.

Let's jump right in and see how this affects the baseline segregation model. Change the model by giving every agent a small probability of making a random move, even when happy?. This probability is an important new model parameter, so declare a new global variable migration-rate by adding a slider to the interface. This specifies a typical percentage of agents who make random migrations to different empty patches, whether or not they are happy?. You can nest the path-dependent baseline model in the extension by setting migration-rate to zero. Now add a new procedure, random-migration:

```
to random-migration
  let n-movers int (count turtles * migration-rate / 100)
  ask n-of (n-movers) turtles [find-new-spot]
end
```

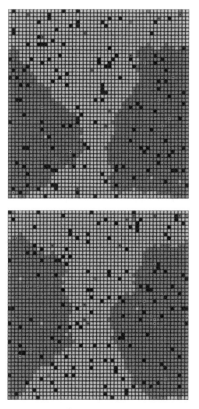

Figure 5.1 Stochastic segregation model; default parameterization and migration-rate = 0.01. NetLogo world at 5,005 iterations (top panel) and 50,005 iterations (bottom panel)

The `let` instruction picks a random number of movers, `n-movers`, multiplying the migration rate by the total number of agents and taking the integer part of the result (dropping anything after the decimal place). Then we pick `n-movers` agents at random and ask them to move, as if they were unhappy – that is, we ask them to make random moves in search of a new empty location. Add this new stochastic component to the model's `go` procedure by inserting `random-migration` before the final `tick` instruction. Save as **Segregation 3 stochastic**, and you're done.

Figure 5.1 shows screenshots of worlds generated by setting `random-migration` at 1 percent and running the model, with all other parameters set to out-of-the box defaults, for just over 5,000 cycles (top panel) and then on to just over 50,000 cycles, (bottom panel). Visually, we see *much* higher levels of evolved social segregation (roughly 94 percent in this case) than for the baseline model with the same settings (which we estimated rigorously at about 75 percent).

Comparing the two segregation maps in Figure 5.1, it's remarkable how similar they look. Not only do they have about the same level of evolved social segregation, despite the continuous churn arising from random migration, but the two geographic configurations of agents' locations even look very similar. We see something new here: a stochastic steady state. Despite continuous movement generated by the model, key outputs of interest effectively stay the same. Each iteration of the model changes these outputs somewhat, but they are not tending to change in any systematic way over the long run. Model outputs appear to have converged, not on a *stationary* state, but on a *stochastic steady state*.

This happens because every agent now has some probability of moving every model cycle. Over a huge number of model cycles, and we will shortly specify a suite of model runs with 100,000 cycles, almost every agent with 1 percent migration probability will be required several times to move to a random new location. We therefore expect this stochastic version of the segregation model to be much less path-dependent than the deterministic versions of the model we worked with in previous sections. Indeed, given the nonzero probability that any agent might move anywhere in the NetLogo world regardless of its starting location, in theory we expect our new model to generate a process that is not path-dependent at all, always converging on the same stochastic steady state over the extremely long run, though always then fluctuating randomly around this.

In this event, we say the stochastic segregation model generates an ergodic process. An ergodic process is one in which the next state of the world depends on the current state of the world, and any logically possible state of the world can occur with some positive probability, however small that probability might be. Ergodic processes are therefore not path-dependent and tend to generate the same distribution of outcomes regardless of the starting point of the process. For obvious reasons this is often a desirable property of an ABM, or indeed any model. We then *in theory* only need a single long-enough model run to map out the stochastic steady state of the process for any given parameter setting. The obvious next question is, how long is long enough? We'll soon find out that this can be a very long time indeed, too long for us to manage feasibly, so that *in practice* we need other ways to characterize model outputs.

We tackle this problem by repeating several very long model runs, each with the same parameterization but a different random starting configuration of agents. We observe the point at which these repetitions converge on the same stochastic steady state – for example, when all repetitions are generating values of percent-similar that vary randomly around the same long-run mean and are not trending up or down. This is a stochastic version of the problem of estimating *model burn-in*. Figure 5.2 reports results of an experiment designed to estimate the length of the burn-in era for the stochastic segregation model with `migration-rate` set to 1 percent and all other parameters at their default values. This involves eight 100,000-cycle repetitions, measuring outputs at every tick, and is experiment 1 in the model **Segregation 3**.

I chose eight long runs rather than, for example, ten for purely practical reasons that have nothing to do with theory or method. The machine I'm using makes eight virtual processing cores available to NetLogo. If I had chosen ten runs, then the machine would have first competed a run on each of the eight virtual cores, then started on the final two. This experiment would have taken twice as long to run for 25 percent more information, a complete waste of computational firepower. If I need more than eight runs in this case, I can have 16 for the price of ten. To get maximum bang for your computational buck – and you *always* want this when doing a lot of computing, especially with a few very long runs – *specify the number of repetitions in multiples of c, where c is the number of virtual cores NetLogo is using*. This little trick gives you a much faster computer for zero dollars.

This experiment takes a long time to run and generates a *lot* of output – 800,000 lines in all – so, sadly, in this case you'll need software other than Google Sheets to hold and analyze it. But it's what we need to investigate whether and how model outputs are converging on a stochastic steady state. The top panel of Figure 5.2 shows the evolution of segregation (`percent-similar`) for the first 5,000 cycles of each repetition; the bottom panel shows this for the final 80,000 cycles of each repetition. Looking first at the top panel, we see an initial very rapid rise, followed by a much slower, but nonetheless relentless increase in `percent-similar`. While model outputs look close to being in steady state, model output is still trending up slightly and the means for each run are slightly different.

The bottom panel of Figure 5.3 shows output for the final 80,000 model cycles of each of the eight repetitions and shows that we *still* have not fully converged, even after 100,000 model cycles, though we are clearly getting closer. The range of the vertical axis is now much smaller, running from 92 to 96 `percent-similar`. Look first at the plots for repetitions 1 and 8, which as we'll soon see are closest to convergence. This is what a stochastic steady state looks like, with chaotic but limited variation around a stationary mean. Repetitions 2 and 7 also look as if they are generating chaotic but limited variation around a stationary mean and, if we only had these to look at, we might think they had converged. But when we compare these plots with those for repetitions 1 and 8, we see that the long-run mean is significantly lower. Furthermore, we know *theoretically* that we have specified a model according to

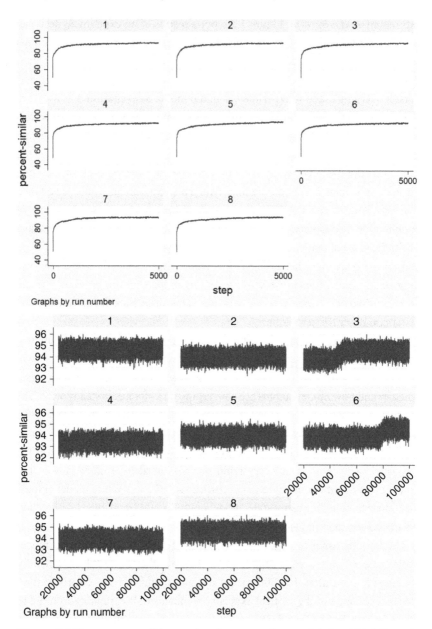

Figure 5.2 Convergence of the stochastic segregation model: 8 × 100,000 cycle repetitions

which, regardless of their random scatter at the start of the run, any agent can potentially occupy any position in the NetLogo world.

Consider any agent A and any new location L. If L is empty, then with some nonzero probability A may be asked to move to L. If L is occupied, then the agent occupying L may with some nonzero probability be asked to leave L, and then with some nonzero probability A may be asked to move there. From any given configuration of the NetLogo world it is theoretically possible, even if extraordinarily unlikely, to attain any other configuration of the NetLogo world. For this reason we know theoretically that the process generated by this model should evolve to be ergodic over the very long run.

Knowing this in theory, we suspect repetitions 2 and 7 have in practice not converged. Repetitions 3 and 6 support this suspicion in a striking and very interesting way. We see a relatively sudden level shift, sometimes called a regime shift, in model output. Repetitions 3 and 6 look like repetitions 2, 5, and 7 for a long time, up to about 80,000 model-cycles for repetition 7. They then suddenly reset to look more like repetitions 1 and 8. We're using "suddenly" here in the evolutionary context of 100,000-cycle run repetitions, since each shift takes place over many thousands of model cycles and would not be observable to the naked eye if you were staring at the screen watching the NetLogo world in motion. Combined with our theoretical expectation of convergence to a single stochastic steady state, this leads us to suspect that repetitions 2, 4, 5, and 7 have yet to experience the type of regime shift we see in repetitions 3 and 6, and therefore have not yet converged.

The regime shifts we observe in repetitions 3 and 6 are both striking and common in the very long-run evolution of stochastic models such as this. What happens is that the model world, just like the real world, gets stuck at a particular point in its evolution. After a long period of relative stability, some random throws of the dice unstick the model and move it to another regime. Evolutionary change does not always happen slowly and steadily, but can happen suddenly after long periods of stability. Imagine, for example, you had a model generating a stable outcome as long as you don't throw 1,000 double-sixes in a row. You might say, and you would *almost* be right, that you will *never* throw 1,000 double-sixes in a row, so your model output will always be stable. On an evolutionary timescale, however, you will indeed eventually throw 1,000 double-sixes in a row and your stable outcome will change. You might, quite reasonably, say in response to this that you don't *care* about the extremely long run, that the real world that interests you operates on a much shorter timescale. In which case you would be saying, though you might not realize this, that you don't care about the long-run convergence of your model outputs. This is a valid point of view, but it does mean you now need a plausible way to characterize typical model outputs when these have not converged on a stochastic steady state. As we will see, there are ways to do this that are not a million miles from what we've already been doing.

Table 5.1 Mean percent-similar, per 10,000-cycle era, per run

	Run								Mean of
Era	1	2	3	4	5	6	7	8	means
0	92.47	92.39	92.15	91.70	92.42	92.06	92.85	93.01	92.38
1	94.64	93.92	93.76	93.38	94.02	93.83	93.85	94.59	94.00
2	94.67	94.03	93.88	93.33	93.98	93.87	93.95	94.64	94.04
3	94.66	94.03	93.86	93.47	93.95	93.90	93.92	94.66	94.06
4	94.64	94.00	94.06	93.45	93.98	93.91	94.03	94.67	94.09
5	94.66	94.05	94.60	93.50	93.96	93.82	93.98	94.68	94.16
6	94.66	94.05	94.67	93.43	93.96	93.85	93.96	94.67	94.15
7	94.65	94.05	94.64	93.48	94.00	93.95	93.99	94.68	94.18
8	94.67	94.08	94.61	93.46	94.00	94.61	93.92	94.67	94.25
9	94.67	94.04	94.61	93.42	93.94	94.63	93.91	94.66	94.24

Returning to Figure 5.2, there's a big lesson for all who model long-term social interaction. Don't just look at one very long model run and declare victory on convergence when you see something like the plot for repetition 4. Do as many repetitions as possible, with as many model cycles as possible before deciding your model outputs are converging. But your time budget is limited and you can't estimate convergence by doing infinite run repetitions of infinite length. So when should you stop? The answer to this question is pragmatic and depends on what it is you want to measure and how accurately you want to measure it.

Table 5.1 presents output from the same eight long diagnostic run repetitions of the stochastic segregation model. We hardly ever look in this Element at model outputs as *numbers*, since most numbers are arbitrary and we are much more interested in the shape of things, but these particular numbers do have a story to tell. I split each 100,000-cycle repetition into ten 10,000-cycle eras and calculated mean percent-similar for each era. I said earlier that repetitions 1 and 8 seemed to have converged and I now confess I said this because I'd already peeked at Table 5.1. If we conjecture that the values of percent-similar for this parametrization of the model will converge on a stochastic steady state with a long-run mean of, say 94.66 or 94.67, then repetitions 1 and 8 hit this mean quite quickly, after a mere 20,000 cycles or so, and essentially oscillate around this thereafter.

Turning to level shifts we saw in repetitions 3 and 6, these are highlighted and clearly visible in Table 5.1. Each shift suddenly (on an evolutionary timescale)

pops the mean up to 94.61 or so, very close to what we see in repetitions 1 and 8. Noting the level shifts in repetitions 3 and 6 and knowing our model should in theory converge on a stochastic steady state, we suspect such shifts remain in store for repetitions 2, 4, 5, and 7.

We still haven't answered the question of how to know when model output has converged. This depends a lot on why you want to measure a typical level of evolved social segregation. Do you need to know this to two decimal places? To one decimal place? Usually, we don't actually care about the *precise* number. What we mostly care about is whether typical values of percent-similar for some parameterization of a model are substantially *different* from typical values arising from different parametrizations of the same model or from the same parameterization of different models. The actual number itself, taken in isolation, is of no intrinsic interest whatsoever. It's just a number. What we care about are *theoretically and substantively important differences in outputs generated by the model in different settings.*

Go back to our very first experiment, reported in Table 3.1, estimating percent-similar for the baseline model, which we now know is path-dependent. We found that, with default settings of 95 for density and 30 for %-similar-wanted, the typical evolved percent-similar is 74.9. We just added a stochastic component and found that, for identical settings of %-similar-wanted and density and a setting of migration-rate of 1 percent, our best estimate of evolved percent-similar is 94.6 or 94.7. This is an important finding. It tells us that adding the continuous random migration of happy? agents *leads to much more social segregation* over the long run, because on any account 94.6 is much bigger than 74.9. Our new model generated a new finding that is not only striking, but theoretically and substantively relevant to our understanding of social segregation. The substantive intuition from the baseline model is that evolved levels of social segregation are much higher than our agents desire. We now see this may well be an *underestimate* of the size of this effect once we take account of the fact that, in the real world, agents may move for reasons that have nothing to do with their social neighborhoods. The model with random migration leads to *much* more segregation than the model without this. We learned something new and interesting, which is the whole point of the exercise. We don't care at all about the precise numbers 74.9 and 94.6, just that one is substantially (and statistically) bigger than the other.

You don't need the world's most perfect estimate of evolved percent-similar when migration-rate is 1 percent, density is 95, and %-similar-wanted is 30. You could get this by running your computer until smoke pours out of it, but that would be completely pointless. What you want is a "good enough" estimate that is fit for purpose, and only you can be the judge of that. For example, those eight diagnostic run repetitions all generate `percent-similar` over 80 after only 100 cycles as opposed to 100,000, and never dip below this. So we know even by then that evolved social segregation is higher with the stochastic model. We also know, having done the full set of diagnostic repetitions, that the 80 percent estimate would have been pretty misleading if we'd stopped at 100 cycles. Looking again at Table 5.1, and in particular at the final column, which shows the mean of the means for each era across all eight repetitions, we see that we're definitely not there by the end of the first era, but we're pretty much there by the second era. So we could, for example, specify a suite of run repetitions that continue to 10,000 cycles, discarding all output up to this point as reflecting a transient state or burn-in of the model en route to its eventual stochastic steady state. This stochastic model is generating what is really quite a long burn-in era. This is not uncommon with stochastic models, though you'll often find models for which "fit for purpose" burn-in occurs much more quickly.

Our intuition might then be to let each run continue for, say, a further 1,000 cycles after burn-in, computing mean `percent-similar` over these 1,000 cycles. However, collecting 1,000 observations of a run repetition that has not fully converged, while not wrong, is not really any better than collecting a single observation in this window. The 1,000 observations are not independent estimates of what we want to measure, which is the typical level of evolved `percent-similar` generated by the model with this parameterization. They all come from the same repetition, which has not yet converged and is still on a distinctive nonconverged path.

We see this by modifying the previous experiment to specify 100 independent 11,000-cycle repetitions of the stochastic model run with `density` set to 95, `%-similar-wanted` to 30, and `migration-rate` to 1 percent. (Warning: this took about 90 minutes on my (fast) laptop and generated 1.1 million lines of output.) Ignore the first 10,000 cycles as burn-in and estimate the typical value of evolved `percent-similar` in two ways. First, for each of the 100 independent repetitions, take the mean of the 1,000 observations for the burnt-in era. Now take the mean of these 100 means. When I did this, the result was 94.04 `percent-similar`. Second, observe `percent-similar` at cycle 10,500 for each of the 100 repetitions (a single cycle in the burnt-in era) and take the mean of these 100 observations. When I did this, the result was 94.00 – pretty much the same as for the previous method. In each case you only really have 100 independent observations, since each of the 100 model run repetitions is still on its own path.

Both methods are correct, in a sense, but collecting only a single observation from the burnt-in era is *much* more efficient computationally, since you're not writing model output to a file after every iteration. You achieve this here by unchecking "Measure outputs at every step" in the BehaviorSpace design window and setting a time limit for each run of 10,500 steps. Each of the 100 model run repetitions generates a single line of output and each run stops 500 steps sooner, so the computational load will be much less. The 100-line output file is *much* more manageable than the 1.1-million-line file generated by the other method, especially since you're going to ignore almost all of the larger file as burn-in.

An efficient way to analyze a stochastic model such as this is first to estimate the length of a burn-in era that is "fit for purpose." Given what you want to estimate, do the costs of a longer burn-in, which typically increase in a linear fashion with length of burn-in, outweigh the benefits, which are typically subject to diminishing marginal returns? Now specify a suite of run repetitions that stop one model cycle into the burnt-in era, recording the output of interest for this first burnt-in model cycle. Complete several (say eight) burnt-in run repetitions for each parameter setting. All of this is just a rule of thumb for efficient use of a fixed computational budget. It trades off fit-for-purpose estimates for a given parameter setting against the benefit of investigating as many parameter settings as possible. You may prefer a different trade-off, but be aware that while specifying huge numbers of massively long runs for a single parameter setting may give you a more precise description of model outputs for this one parameterization, it is almost never the best use of your computer's time.

Returning to our stochastic model of social segregation, we already saw that the stochastic model with out-of-the-box parameter settings and a `migration-rate` set to 1 percent generates levels of segregation that evolve to be much higher than for the baseline path-dependent model. What interests us now is whether the new stochastic parameter, `migration-rate`, systematically affects levels of evolved social segregation. We investigate this by designing an experiment with multiple 10,000-cycle burnt-in run repetitions that sweep values of `migration-rate` between 0.5 and 5.0, setting `density` at 90 percent to speed convergence but keeping `%-similar-wanted` at 30. This is experiment 2 in model **Segregation 3**. Speeding convergence in this case will not result in shorter repetitions, since we have settled on a burn-in era of 10,000 cycles as fit for purpose. However, it does mean that our repetitions should be closer to convergence by the time they reach 10,000 cycles.

It's easy to see logically that, if the `migration-rate` is 100 percent, then `percent-similar` must on average be 50. Everybody is moving all of the time to random locations so, since 50 percent of agents come from each group, it

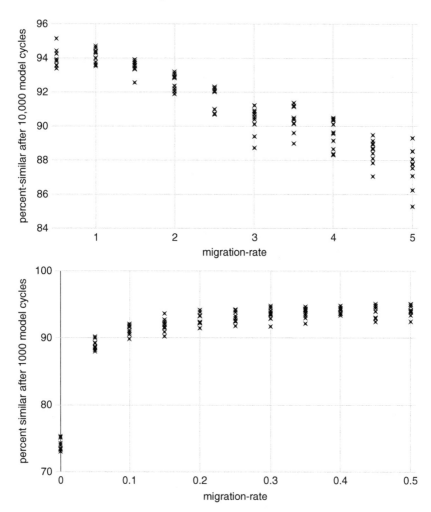

Figure 5.3 Evolved percent-similar for different migration rates

must be the case that on average 50 percent of every agent's neighbors come from the same group. So we know theoretically that, in the limit, evolved `percent-similar` will approach 50 as `migration-rate` approaches its maximum.

The top panel of Figure 5.3 reports results from an experiment specifying 10 repetitions each, for settings of `migration-rate` increasing in 0.5 percent intervals from 0.5 to 5.0, making a total of 100 run repetitions, each of 10,000 cycles. This shows that evolved `percent-similar` declines steadily as `migration-rate` increases, as expected, though to nowhere near 50 percent within the range of `migration-rate` we investigate. We also see widely varying values of `percent-similar` for higher settings of `migration-`

rate. Since we know theoretically that this process should be ergodic on an evolutionary time scale, this suggests model outputs are converging more slowly for higher values of migration-rate. We also see that the highest values of evolved social segregation are associated with a migration-rate of 1 percent. Whether this was good or bad luck, the default setting of our stochastic migration parameter happens to be associated with the strongest segregation effects.

We also know from our earlier experiments that if we set migration-rate at zero, nesting the baseline model, then percent-similar typically evolves to about 74–75 percent. This means it must pop up very quickly for low but nonzero levels of migration-rate, since it hits 94 percent by the time migration-rate is 1 percent. We check this out in another experiment, reported in the bottom panel of Figure 5.3, which sweeps settings of migration-rate in the range of 0 to 0.5 percent, in increments of 0.05. This shows us clearly that shifting migration-rate from zero to 0.05 percent, allowing even a tiny amount of random migration, results in a huge increase in evolved percent-similar. By the time migration-rate is 0.1 percent, typical evolved levels of social segregation are close to their maximum values. This is an important lesson. Adding a new stochastic component to our model, especially to a model otherwise generating path-dependent outcomes, can make a big difference.

If we've taken to heart the lessons we learned in the previous section, however, we'll know that we're not nearly done at this stage. In particular, since we introduced an important new model parameter, migration-rate, we're sensitive to the possibility that it may *interact* with other crucial model parameters, in particular %-similar-wanted. Although the long burn-in era means this is going to take a lot of computer time, we design an experiment manipulating both migration-rate and %-similar-wanted. Because we want to present our three-dimensional results graphically, plotting output for particular settings of migration-rate and %-similar-wanted, we design our experiment as a grid sweep. In the "Vary variables" pane, therefore, we specify ["migration-rate" [1 1 5]] and ["%-similar-wanted" [30 10 60]], and ask for 8 burnt-in repetitions of 10,000 cycles for each of the 5 × 4 = 20 model parameterizations that result. This 160-repetition experiment involves 1.6 million model cycles and will take about an hour to run on a good laptop, generating a mere 160 observations of interest. But they will be 160 good observations from burnt-in model run repetitions, observations from which we will be confident in drawing inferences. (There is nothing to stop you from running this experiment overnight if you crave more observations.)

Migration rates, from top to bottom = 1, 2, 3, 4, 5%

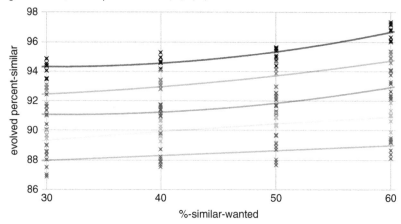

Figure 5.4 Evolved percent-similar by migration-rate and %-similar-wanted

We could drastically shorten the burn-in era and collect many more observations, but these would be from repetitions we know are still trending and therefore do not represent model outputs in a stochastic steady state. It is difficult to know what inferences we could draw from such observations. This is the agent-based modeling version of a fundamental scientific principle: a small number of good observations is much better than a large number of bad ones.

Figure 5.4 plots the relationship between %-similar-wanted and evolved percent-similar for different levels of migration-rate. Results arising from different migration rates, and trend lines summarizing these, are plotted in different colors. We know from the top panel of Figure 5.3 that evolved percent-similar declines as the migration-rate increases past 1 percent. Figure 5.4 confirms this; the trend lines drop as migration-rate increases. We also see this decline for each level of %-similar-wanted we investigate.

Figure 3.10 showed that evolved percent-similar increases as %-similar-wanted increases. Comparing Figures 5.3 and 3.10, we saw that evolved percent-similar tends to be substantially higher once we introduce the possibility of random migration by happy? agents, suggesting that the results from the baseline Schelling segregation model are, if anything, an underestimate. Figure 5.4 confirms that these results all hold once we manipulate %-similar-wanted and migration-rate at the same time; we introduce no new and unexpected interaction effects when we do this.

Figure 5.3 therefore gives us the headline news about the effects of adding a stochastic component to the model by introducing the possibility of random moves by `happy?` agents. This makes a big difference. Even small values of `migration-rate` substantially change the well-known conclusions from the baseline Schelling segregation model. Intuitively this is because, when `happy?` agents move, some of these will be just barely `happy?`. One fewer similar neighbor would make them sad. They keep moving until they find another spot that makes them `happy?` Sometimes this will also make them just barely `happy?`, but more often than not it will leave them with a greater proportion of similar neighbors than they need to make them `happy?`. While this may not be obvious at first sight we can now see that, iterated over and over again, this part of the segregation process results in even higher levels of evolved `percent-similar` than those arising in the path-dependent baseline model with no random migration. This, I think, is a valuable new intuition.

Adding this stochastic component to the Schelling segregation model makes it more realistic. It makes *substantive* sense to model a world in which some people move home for reasons that have nothing to do with the social composition of their local neighborhood. It also seems substantively implausible to model a world in which, once all agents find locations that make them happy, nobody moves again for the rest of eternity.

This stochastic component also improves our model *methodologically*. Before adding a small number of moves by even happy agents, the Schelling segregation model was clearly path-dependent. Where it stops depends on where it starts. After adding this random noise to the model, outputs of interest can never stop at a stationary state, though they can converge on a stochastic steady state in which they continue to vary around a stationary long-term mean. The stochastic steady state is the same no matter where the model starts.

We achieved this not just by adding any old stochastic component, for example, by allowing agents to give themselves random silly names. Our core output of interest is the configuration of agent locations. We added a stochastic component with the critical effect that any agent has some probability, even if this is extremely small, of moving to any location in the NetLogo world. We know logically that this means that any model run can – on an evolutionary timescale, and regardless of the initial scatter of agents' locations – generate any configuration of agent locations. Model outputs can evolve after burn-in to be ergodic rather than path-dependent, so that very long runs tend to generate the same distributions of outputs. This is a nice property. However, since nice things usually come at a cost, we pay for this with suites of experiments that consume substantially more computer time. As we just saw, this price is worth paying because the results we generate are quite different from the more tractable, but path-dependent and less realistic baseline Schelling segregation model.

6 Trading Realism against Intuition

We've come a long way in using ABMs to help us understand social segregation. We built on Schelling's seminal model, as implemented in the NetLogo models library. We moved beyond simply *playing* with this model to interrogate it systematically and use it to generate *reproducible findings* that others can take seriously. We identified *implicit model parameters* lurking in the code, dragging these out into plain sight and investigating their effects. We *generalized key features of the model*, such as the number of social groups and the size of social neighborhoods. And we added an important *stochastic component*, the random migration of happy agents, reflecting the inescapable fact that agents in the real world behave in ways that have nothing to do with the model, however good the model might be. We made all of these improvements to the model one at a time to allow us to get a good sense of their individual effects. In this final section we do something that seems both natural and ambitious. We implement a whole set of realistic modifications to the segregation model at the same time. This is actually very easy to do with an agent-based model. Easy, but dangerous – very dangerous.

We face a fundamental tension between realism and intuition when we model social interaction and indeed most other things. We want our model to be as close to the real world as possible. Making a model more realistic means adding more features. Adding more features, however, typically makes it much harder to get to grips with exactly how the model works. When a model has only one key feature, we can manipulate this in a systematic way to investigate its effects on outputs of interest. This is easy to understand but unrealistic. We already saw that adding just one more feature to make a model more realistic makes it not only more taxing to investigate in a systematic way but more difficult to understand. It's not just that we need to manipulate two features at once, separating independent effects of these in our analysis. But effects of two features often *interact*; effects of feature A may depend on settings of feature B. Making the model even more realistic by adding even more features, and *many* more possible interactions, vastly complicates this problem.

In what follows we'll get a good sense of this when we specify a more realistic extended version of the Schelling segregation model that has *six* sliders on the interface, setting six key global parameters. Focusing only on pairwise interactions between variables gives 30 possible interactions between pairs of variables as well as the 6 variables themselves. We now have 36 things to worry about, even before considering potential interactions between groups of three, four, or five variables. Quite apart from the massive computational load needed to map out all possible interactions for a stochastic model with a long burn-in era, drawing useful general intuitions from all of this will be beyond most humans, and certainly beyond me. Increasing the model's realism in this way paradoxically reduces its value as an aid to *intuition*.

On the other hand, we may want to use a model to make reliable *predictions* about the real world, even if we don't fully understand these. The problem now is quite different. We no longer really care about how the model behaves for all possible parameter settings, for all possible realizations of the world. What we care about now is what our model predicts in a few real-world cases that interest us. Our problem now is one of finding the right parameter settings for these cases – of calibrating our model to real-world situations of interest. The difficulties we face when trying to calibrate our models typically arise because some parameters are latent quantities that we can never observe directly. Take the crucial `%-similar-wanted` parameter in the baseline Schelling segregation model, for example. If people had this quantity tattooed on their foreheads, then measuring it for a given population would not be hard. But this is a deeply latent quantity that exists somewhere in each person's (quite possibly subconscious) brain. It's not at all clear, for example, how we might come up with a reliable and valid calibration of the value `%-similar-wanted` for the residents of New York City or London in 2019.

A More Realistic Multifeature Model of Social Segregation

As always, we get a better sense of the problems that confront us by getting our hands dirty, in this case specifying a more realistic model of social segregation by adding several of the features we considered in previous sections. Let's say we want our "all-singing, all-dancing" model of social segregation to have the following features.

1. **Stochastic**. Not only is the real world characterized by pervasive uncertainties but modeling these uncertainties can change our findings in fundamental ways. We therefore add a stochastic component involving the random migration of even `happy?` agents, with a probability specified by the parameter `migration-rate`.
2. **Multiple occupancy of patches**. The real world is characterized by multiple occupancy of some housing locations, resulting in substantial variations in housing densities. We therefore remove the baseline model's restriction that there can only be one agent per patch. There is no explicit parameter associated with this extension, though there is an implicit parameter

specifying the maximum occupancy of any patch. By not specifying this, we implicitly allow all agents in our model world to occupy the same patch, if that is what they choose to do. It would, however, be very simple to add an additional parameter for maximum occupancy, modeling legislation that regulates multiple occupancy, if this interests you.

3. **More than two social groups.** The real world involves more than two social groups. We therefore modify the model to allow any number of social groups, adding the associated model parameter n-groups. We do not deviate from the baseline modeling assumption that all groups are, on average, the same size. It would be easy, though messy, since it would involve adding n-groups – 1 new parameters to specify the relative size of each group. You should try this if it interests you.

4. **Agent-specific %-similar-wanted**. Real humans from the same social group are not all clones of each other. We model this by making %-similar-wanted, which captures preferences for having neighbors from the same group, an agent-specific rather than a global variable. For each agent, we draw the value of %-similar-wanted from a normal distribution specified by two new model parameters, mean-sim-wanted and sd-sim-wanted.

5. **Agent-specific neighborhood sizes**. Real humans do not all think the same about the size of their social neighborhood. We therefore modify the model in a new way to make the radius of social neighborhoods, nabe, an agent-specific rather than a global variable. A simple way to do this is for each agent to pick a random integer for neighborhood radius, between 1 and a new model parameter, max-nabe. We make this happen by adding set nabe 1 + random max-nabe to the code run by each agent immediately after it is created. Note that when max-nabe is set to 2, for each agent this is either 1 or 2, representing a hyperlocal choice between von Neumann and Moore neighborhoods. This is another example of generalizing a model feature, which for simplicity we begin by treating as a global parameter, by making the more realistic assumption that it is really a feature of individual agents – but then facing decisions about how it varies between agents.

Put all this together and the result is a model of social segregation that in many ways looks more realistic than the baseline Schelling model. This is **Segregation 4 all singing, all dancing**, with an interface that looks like the screenshot in Figure 6.1. This particular model run, with parameter settings shown on the interface sliders, was allowed to continue for over 10,000 cycles, with agent locations evolving into the configuration shown in Figure 6.1.

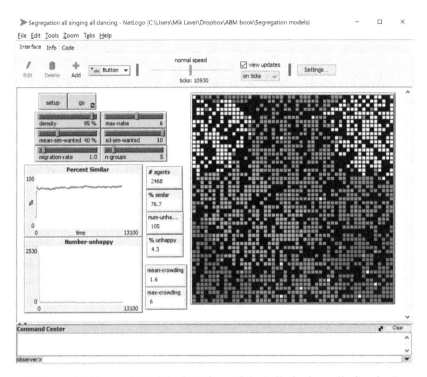

Figure 6.1 Screenshot of the interface of the "all-singing, all- dancing" segregation model

Play with this model and you quickly find out that, with the effects of six parameters and their potential interactions to keep track of, it's really hard to get a good sense of what's going on, much harder than when we changed one parameter at a time in a systematic way. Holding everything else constant and referring to our earlier findings, Figure 4.8 suggests that increasing `max-nabe` should reduce evolved `percent-similar`, while Figures 4.15 and 4.16 suggest that increasing `sd-sim-wanted` should have no effect on this. Figure 4.17 suggests that increasing `n-groups` should tend to increase evolved `percent-similar`, while Figure 5.4 suggests that increasing `migration-rate` above 0.1 should tend to reduce this. I frankly have no well-founded idea about how these variables *interact* with each other to influence evolved levels of social segregation. Yet, comparing Figures 4.11 and 4.12, we see they certainly can interact, with completely different shapes of the relationship between neighborhood radius and evolved `percent-similar` for different values of `%-similar-wanted`. Mapping all this out in a rigorous way would take a huge amount of carefully designed computational work. Since we have a stochastic model that, as we will soon see, takes a long time to burn in, this will generate a massive computational load.

We might crave a supercomputer, but this is not the real problem. Even if we did all necessary computational work on our supercomputer, results will be extremely difficult to synthesize into important take-home intuitions about social segregation, analogous to those we drew from the baseline model and simple one-feature extensions of this. At the end of the day, a more realistic and complicated model such as this may do little to enhance our understanding about the social process we are modeling. This problem is not confined in any way to agent-based modeling – it's a pervasive problem facing everyone who sets out to develop theoretical models of the real world. Ultimately, as far as intuitions are concerned, simpler models are better.

However, a more realistic but complicated model may have an important use beyond giving us intuitions. Imagine your main concern is with a particular real-world case of social segregation *and* that you chose the parameter settings shown in Figure 6.1 because these were your best calibration of parameters for this case. Now what you want to do is to use the model to get the best possible *prediction* of evolved levels of social segregation. You may care very little about *understanding* model interactions underlying this prediction; you just care about the prediction. This is a *completely* different job of work. First, knowing that it is a stochastic model, you need to figure out how long the output of interest, evolved percent-similar, takes to burn in for these particular parameter settings. Then, for those same settings, you conduct a suite of burnt-in repetitions, collecting the first burnt-in observation of percent-similar and averaging these as your prediction.

Figure 6.2 shows evolved percent-similar for eight long (25,000-cycle) repetitions of a model run parametrized as in Figure 6.1. This is experiment 1 in the model Segregation 4. The top panel shows results for cycles, 1,000–10,000. We see percent-similar still clearly trending upward for all repetitions. The bottom panel shows results for cycles 10,000–25,000. We see what appear to be eight nontrending stochastic steady states. Echoing our findings in the previous section on burn-in for our stochastic model, we conclude that burn-in is good enough for our purposes at around 10,000 model cycles and specify a suite of 10,000-cycle repetitions.

Given this, we can derive a reliable estimate for evolved percent-similar, for the model parametrization in Figure 6.1. After 72 repetitions of 10,000 cycles each were conducted with this model parameterization, mean evolved percent-similar was 77.1 and the standard deviation of this mean was 0.98, reflecting the fact that the model predictions were typically in the range 75–79 percent-similar. Going back to Figure 3.7, evolved percent-similar arising from the baseline model when %-similar-wanted is 40 is about 83–84 percent (83.4 percent for these repetitions, to be

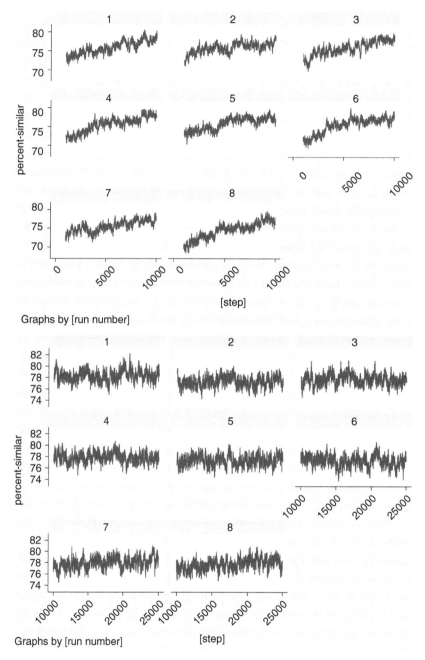

Figure 6.2 Evolved percent-similar for model cycles 1,000–10,000 (top panel)
and 10,000–25,000 (bottom panel); parameter settings as in Figure 6.1

The BehaviorSpace specification was ["migration-rate" 1] ["mean-sim-wanted"
40] ["density" 95] ["n-groups" 5] ["max-nabe" 6] ["sd-sim-wanted" 10]

precise, with a standard deviation of 0.90). In other words, the more realistic model predicts *substantially lower levels of social segregation than the baseline model*, although still far higher levels than agents actually want. However, we have no good sense from any of this about what, precisely, it is about this more complex model that underlies this finding. In terms of understanding social segregation, the fancier model has yet to help us. We need to start moving several parameters at the same time, in systematic ways, and mapping out the results.

Multivariate Simulations and Analysis

Now that we have an "all-singing, all-dancing" segregation model that allows us to modify several features at the same time, we must think hard about how best to exercise it is a systematic way. In what follows, to keep things simple, we decide we want a stochastic model but are not at this stage interested in effects of varying migration-rate. We settle on a fixed value of 1 percent for this and focus attention on the potentially interacting effects of three other key model features: the number of different groups, the size of social neighborhoods, and the number of similar neighbors it takes to make agents happy?. To keep things simple, and painfully aware there are many more complex simulation designs and analyses we could specify, we settle on three values of each of these parameters. These are: for n-groups, 2, 6, and 10; for max-nabe, 2, 6, and10; and for mean-sim-wanted 30, 40, and 50. We fix density at 95 percent and sd-sim-wanted at 10. This design gives $3 \times 3 \times 3 = 27$ different parameterizations of our stochastic model. You may well be banging the table and shouting that a different experimental design makes much more sense. My reply is that this is *exactly* what you should be thinking. Please design, run, and analyze as many different experiments as interest you. This is *precisely* why we're doing all this.

For now, however, since we're working with run repetitions with a burn-in era estimated as good enough at 10,000 cycles, we specify only 10 run repetitions per parameterization, 270 repetitions in all, each of 10,000 cycles. This experiment is experiment 2 in the model **Segregation 3**. It took several hours on my high-spec laptop to complete – precisely how long I don't know, because I went to bed and woke up to find it finished. A wonderful aspect of ABM work is that you can make excellent progress even when you're sleeping.

Thus far we have manipulated one model feature to affect one model output and displayed results using a two-dimensional graph, following the convention of plotting model features on the horizontal axis and model outputs on the vertical. With three model features and one model output, we need either a four-

Table 6.1 Mean evolved percent-similar, by mean-sim-wanted, n-groups and max-nabe. Migration-rate = 0.01, density = 95, sd-sim-wanted = 10

%-similar-wanted		n-groups	max-nabe	
		2	**6**	**10**
30				
	2	88.4	75.5	63.6
	6	80.5	64.9	56.4
	10	74.5	60.7	49.5
40				
	2	93.5	85.0	78.7
	6	85.7	74.9	66.9
	10	80.7	10.0	10.0
50				
	2	96.5	90.3	86.0
	6	88.4	16.6	16.7
	10	16.1	10.1	10.0

dimensional graph or to do things differently. This is another reason I specified a coarse grid sweep as a first sketch of these relationships, with only three values per model parameter, since it's then possible to report results in the type of four-dimensional table you see in Table 6.1. The table cells show model output, mean evolved percent-similar (which would be "height above the page" if this were a graph), for the 27 model parameterizations investigated, arranged in three two-way tables. These are like three slices of a three-dimensional plot. The top, middle, and bottom panels show, for three values of %-similar-wanted (30, 40, 50), the effect of the other two model parameters on evolved percent-similar.

The biggest news in Table 6.1 is a major discontinuity in the results, analogous to discontinuities identified in Section 4 (Figures 4.10 and 4.12). Such discontinuities are always possible in complex systems like our "all-singing, all-dancing" segregation model and are highlighted in the bottom right of the middle and lower panels in Table 6.1. Once again, the suddenly very low numbers of evolved percent-similar arise because we hit a computational wall when constraints on every agent being happy? become extraordinarily hard to satisfy. This happens when max-nabe is 6 or over, n-groups is 10, and %-similar-wanted is 40 or over. For the larger neighborhood sizes and 10 groups it is for all practical purposes impossible to find a configuration that makes all agents happy? when %-similar-

`wanted` is 40 or more. Agent locations continue to churn relentlessly in search of this. Evolved `percent-similar` remains at about 10 percent and is effectively the same after 10,000 iterations as it was with the initial random scatter of 10 groups. A similar discontinuity can be seen for larger neighborhood sizes with 6 groups and `%-similar-wanted` at 50; evolved `percent-similar` is then the same, at 16.7, as in the initial random scatter. Again, we see results that are not just nonlinear but show sharp discontinuities, with the discontinuities arising from interactions between the three model variables we investigate.

Apart from these striking discontinuities, Table 6.1 shows substantial continuous effects of model variables. Indeed, if we had only exercised the model by setting `%-similar-wanted` at 30, generating the results reported in the top panel of Table 6.1, we might have concluded that model effects were all neatly continuous. We would have been blind to the discontinuities shown in the bottom of this table, lurking behind uninvestigated parameter settings and waiting to bite us.

Even so, we see that these continuous effects differ from those we saw when manipulating only one model feature at a time. Read *across* the rows of the top panel of Table 6.1 to see that evolved `percent-similar` not only falls as `max-nabe` increases, for all values of `n-groups`, but falls by the same amount. This is consistent with bivariate findings reported in Section 4 (Figure 4.8). However, reading *down* the columns of the top panel we see that evolved `percent-similar` not only *falls* as `n-groups` increases, for all values of `max-nabe`, but falls by the same amount. This is *not* consistent with bivariate findings reported in Section 4 (Figure 4.17), which shows evolved `percent-similar` *rising* with `n-groups` in this range. Something about the interactions in our more complex model has reversed this effect.

Looking at Table 6.1 is an easy way to get a rough sense of some of the interactions between features in our model. We could dig much more deeply into these by designing a much more fine-grained and extensive suite of simulations. We could, for example, specify a finer-grained grid sweep involving a wider range of settings for model features of interest. Thus we could investigate: `%-similar-wanted` in the range 30–80, in increments of 1; `max-nabe` in the range 2–30, in increments of 1; and `n-groups` in the range 2–50, in increments of 1. Or we could specify Monte Carlo parameterizations of these variables with the same general effect. With 51 different parameterizations of `%-similar-wanted`, 29 parametrizations of `max-nabe`, and 49 parameterizations of `n-groups`, we would have $51 \times 29 \times 49 = 72{,}471$ different model parameterizations. This is about 2684 times as many as the model runs reported in Table 6.1, which took several hours on my laptop. On my rough calculations it would take over a year to run. At the end of this, or faster if you get access to some heavy-duty computational muscle, you'd have a beautiful file of results. This would allow you to use sophisticated techniques of multivariate analysis to tease out more complex interactions between model features – if, that is, this is how you want to spend your time. Please don't let me stop you!

The bottom line in all of this is that we build models either to improve our understanding of the world or to make predictions about states of the world in certain well-described circumstances. When weather forecasters tell us when and where on the coastline they expect a hurricane to hit, they're deploying awesome computer power to analyze a tremendously complex and powerful model of the world, with thousands of more-or-less well-measured parameters, *to make a detailed prediction about a particular setting at a particular time.* Most of us will be much more interested in the accuracy of the prediction than with understanding the inner workings of the model, which will be incomprehensible to innocent bystanders. When we model social interactions, however, we are typically more interested in *understanding* what is going on than in making a precise prediction in a particular setting. Aware of the possibility of complex interactions between model features, we try to keep the number of model features and hence interactions as small as possible, consistent with the model adding to our understanding and intuition. Furthermore, we don't necessarily need very *precise* output from our models to get a sense of what is going on. We want to get a sense of what is happening to model output Y when we manipulate model features A and B (and maybe also C), but never need to know this to two decimal places.

Speaking personally, and you may well feel the same way, I learned far more about social segregation from the simple models in Sections 2–5 than I did from the "all-singing, all-dancing" model in this section. Rather than spend more time estimating outputs from simple models more precisely or exercising more complex models in more sophisticated ways, I'd much rather devote that time to working on new agent-based models.

I encourage you to do this right now, and I do this myself in a follow-up Element dealing with models that extend the firepower of agent-based modeling in a number of ways. We'll model how agents' preferences themselves evolve as a result of social interaction rather than treating these as fixed inputs to the model. We'll model how agents interact on social networks. And we'll model a "survival of the fittest" evolutionary environment that allows us to investigate the relative effectiveness of different decision rules that different agents might use in the same setting. For now, however, I'll be more than happy if you feel both eager and able to start building agent-based models of social interactions that really interest you.

Cambridge Elements ☰

Quantitative and Computational Methods for the Social Sciences

R. Michael Alvarez
California Institute of Technology
R. Michael Alvarez has taught at the California Institute of Technology
his entire career, focusing on elections, voting behavior, election technology,
and research methodologies. He has written or edited a number of books
(recently, *Computational Social Science: Discovery and Prediction*, and *Evaluating
Elections: A Handbook of Methods and Standards*) and numerous academic articles
and reports.

Nathaniel Beck
New York University
Nathaniel Beck is Professor of Politics at NYU (and Affiliated Faculty at the NYU Center
for Data Science) where he has been since 2003; before which he was Professor
of Political Science at the University of California, San Diego. He is the founding editor
of the quarterly, *Political Analysis*. He is a fellow of both the American Academy of Arts
and Sciences and the Society for Political Methodology.

About the Series
The Elements Series *Quantitative and Computational Methods for the Social Sciences*
contains short introductions and hands-on tutorials to innovative methodologies.
These are often so new that they have no textbook treatment or no detailed
treatment on how the method is used in practice. Among emerging areas of interest
for social scientists, the series presents machine learning methods, the use of new
technologies for the collection of data and new techniques for assessing causality
with experimental and quasi-experimental data.

Cambridge Elements $^{\equiv}$

Quantitative and Computational Methods for the Social Sciences

Elements in the Series

Twitter as Data
Zachary C. Steinert-Threlkeld

A Practical Introduction to Regression Discontinuity Designs: Foundations
Matias D. Cattaneo, Nicolás Idrobo and Rocío Titiunik

Agent-Based Models of Social Life: Fundamentals
Michael Laver

Agent-Based Models of Polarization and Ethnocentrism
Michael Laver

A full series listing is available at: www.cambridge.org/QCMSS